Canada's Guns

Staff editor: Viviane Appleton
Index: John Swettenham
Production supervisor: Donald Matheson
Design: Gregory Gregory Limited
Typesetting: Typographic Service Limited
Printing: Dollco Printing Limited

**Canada's Guns
An Illustrated History of Artillery**

Canadian War Museum
Historical Publication No. 15

Leslie W.C.S. Barnes

623.409
Bar

National Museum of Man
National Museums of Canada

© National Museums of Canada 1979

Published by the
Canadian War Museum
National Museum of Man
National Museums of Canada
Ottawa, Canada K1A 0M8

Catalogue No. NM95-16/15

Printed in Canada

ISBN 0-660-00137-3

Édition française
Histoire illustrée de l'artillerie canadienne
ISBN 0-660-00138-1

Canadian War Museum Historical Publications
General Editor: John Swettenham

Previous publications in the series:
[1] *Canada and the First World War*, by John Swettenham. Canadian War Museum, Ottawa, 1968. Bilingual.
[2] *D-Day*, by John Swettenham. Canadian War Museum, Ottawa, 1969. Bilingual.
[3] *Canada and the First World War*, by John Swettenham. Based on the Fiftieth Anniversary Armistice Display at the Canadian War Museum. Ryerson, Toronto, 1969. Published in paperback by McGraw-Hill Ryerson, 1973.
[4] *Canadian Military Aircraft*, by J.A. Griffin. Queen's Printer, Ottawa, 1969. Bilingual.
 5 *The Last War Drum: The North West Campaign of 1885*, by Desmond Morton. Hakkert, Toronto, 1972.
 6 *The Evening of Chivalry*, by John Swettenham. National Museums of Canada, Ottawa, 1972. Édition française: *Le crépuscule de la chevalerie*.
 7 *Valiant Men: Canada's Victoria Cross and George Cross Winners*, ed. by John Swettenham. Hakkert, Toronto, 1973.
 8 *Canada Invaded, 1775–1776*, by George F.G. Stanley. Hakkert, Toronto, 1973. Édition française: *L'invasion du Canada*. Société historique de Québec, Québec, 1975.
 9 *The Canadian General, Sir William Otter*, by Desmond Morton. Hakkert, Toronto, 1974.
10 *Silent Witnesses*, by John Swettenham and Herbert F. Wood. Hakkert, Toronto, 1974. Édition française: *Témoins silencieux*, adapté par Jacques Gouin.
11 *Broadcast from the Front: Canadian Radio Overseas in the Second World War*, by A.E. Powley. Hakkert, Toronto, 1975.
12 *Canada's Fighting Ships*, by K.R. Macpherson. Samuel Stevens Hakkert & Co., Toronto, 1975.
13 *Canada's Nursing Sisters*, by G.W.L. Nicholson. Samuel Stevens Hakkert & Co., Toronto, 1975.
14 *RCAF: Squadron Histories and Aircraft, 1924–1968*, by Samuel Kostenuk and John Griffin. Samuel Stevens Hakkert & Co., Toronto, 1977.

To the memory of my father, William Barnes

Sources of Illustrations
I am grateful to the following individuals, institutions and publishers for allowing me to use the illustrations reproduced in this book. Plates 69, 76, 81 and 82 are from my own collection.

Alte Pinakothek, Munich: 2

Ballantine Books, New York: 35*, 46, 66, 67, 68, 70*, 71* (reprinted from John Batchelor and Ian Hogg, *Artillery*, 1973, pp. 14, 145, 91, 91, 91, 100, 100, respectively), 72 (reprinted from Constantine FitzGibbon, *London's Burning*, 1970, p. 71)

Canadian War Museum, Ottawa: 1, 6, 8, 9, 10, 16, 20, 21*, 23 (reprinted from John Muller, *A Treatise of Artillery*, 3rd ed., London, 1780, frontispiece), 25, 27*, 28, 30, 31/32*, 36, 37, 38, 39, 40, 42, 45, 52, 57, 58, 61, 63, 64, 65, 73, 78, 79

Department of National Defence, Ottawa: 44*, 59, 60*

E.P. Publishing Ltd., East Ardsley, England: 3, 4, 5 (reprinted from Sir Ralph Payne-Gallwey, *The Projectile-Throwing Engines of the Ancients*, 1973, pp. 12, 21, 28, respectively; reprinted from the 1907 London edition)

Fort Battleford National Historic Park, Sask.: 33

Hamlyn Publishing Group Ltd., London: 17 (drawing by John Batchelor for I.V. Hogg, *A History of Artillery*, 1974, p. 35)

Her Majesty's Stationery Office, London: 7, 47*, 48, 51, 53

Imperial War Museum, London: 43, 50, 54, 77

General E.M.D. Leslie, Ottawa: 55

Mary Evans Picture Library, London: 11 (reprinted from Louis Figuier, *Merveilles de la science*, 4 vols., Paris, 1867–70)

Parker Gallery, London: 41

Public Archives of Canada, Ottawa: 14, 15, 26, 49, 56, 62, 74, 75, 80

Rotunda Museum, Royal Artillery Institution, Woolwich, England: 13 (reprinted from A.S. Fraser, "Notebook on Laboratory Work", 1828, manuscript in the Institution's library), 18, 22, 29

Royal Canadian Artillery Museum, Shilo, Man.: 34

St. Lawrence Parks Commission, Kingston, Ont.: 24

Stackpole Books, Harrisburg, Pa.: 12* (reprinted from H.L. Peterson, *Round Shot and Rammers*, 1969, p. 26)

*Adapted or redrawn by Gregory Gregory Limited, Ottawa, who also did the drawing numbered 19

Contents

Foreword 9

Preface 11

Prologue 13

**1 "The Final Arbiter of Kings":
The Prehistory of the Gun** 15
Sticks and Stones 16
"The Devil's Invention" 18
Siege Warfare 19
Guns Take to the Field 22
The Art and Craft of Gun-Making 23
"A Black Powder That Kills with
   Much Noise" 25
Projectiles Plain and Fancy 26

**2 The Struggle for Canada:
Gunnery in the Age of Reason** 29
The Swamps and Forests of Canada 30
Coastal Defence and Siege Warfare 30
A King Effects a Revolution 34
Ballistics, the Science of Gunnery 39
The Right Honourable Board 42

**3 The War of 1812 and After:
The Age of Invention** 45
The Invader Repelled 46
Invention in the Field: Shrapnel and Others 47
Congreve and His Rockets 51
Rifling and Breech-Loading: Armstrong
   and Whitworth 52
The Demise of the Smooth-Bore: Palliser 55
Steel Barrels and Anti-Recoil Devices 59
Propellants, Projectiles and High Explosives 60
New Calibres and Carriages 62

4 Canada Abroad: Science Goes to War 65
The Gun of the Western Front 66
The Lessons of the Boer War 66
A New Gun At Last 68
War in the Mud 70
Shell Rationing and the Deadly Prematures 75
The Beginnings of Canada's Arms Industry 76
A Renaissance in Siege Warfare 77
A Brilliant Canadian Lieutenant-Colonel 81

**5 Peace and Yet Another War:
Canada Comes of Age** 85
Canada's Industrial Miracle 86
Between Wars: A New Artillery Piece 87
More New Artillery 90
New Targets: The Tank 91
New Targets: The Aeroplane 98
Coastal Defence 100
The Perfection of Rocketry 101
Propellants, Projectiles and Ever-Higher
   Explosives 102
Canada: Arms Factory to the Free World 104

Suggested Reading List 109

Index 110

Foreword

It gives me a special pleasure to write the foreword for this book. As a gunner before, during and after the Second World War, I have had a long personal association with artillery, so it is not surprising that a book of this kind seems to me to be timely. There is a need for a publication describing the development of gunnery from earliest times, with special attention given to Canada.

The author's knowledge of his subject and his ability to present the information have produced excellent reading. Technical matters have been treated in terms that are comprehensible to the layman. The text and illustrations will appeal to the general reader as well as to past and present members of the Canadian forces. I am sure that artillerymen, in particular, will welcome the book.

Artillery has played a significant role in Canada's history for more than three centuries, a role that should not be forgotten. This book will help serve as a reminder.

Allan Bruce McKinnon, PC, MC, CD, MP
*Minister of National Defence
and Minister of Veterans Affairs*

Editor's Note

To convert the names of British guns—for example, 6-pounders, 18-pounders, and so on—to accord with the metric system would be wrong. The famous 18-pounder field gun of the First World War is known to Canadians and to history as such, and the metric equivalent would be confusing. Similarly, the range of these weapons and their weights have not been converted. However, the names and capabilities of foreign guns, such as the famous *soixante-quinze*, are of course expressed in metric.

Preface

Careful study of the great tapestry of struggle and achievement that is Canada's history will identify the guns that played such an important part in shaping our national destiny. This little book will have achieved its primary purpose if it serves as a lens for examining a few of these weapons and encourages readers to broaden their study with the aid of more powerful instruments. I hope that it will also assist visitors to the Canadian War Museum, especially students, to link some of the artillery weapons and related artifacts displayed there with the great events in which they played such an important part. To this end many of the photographs in this book are of actual exhibits in the Museum. Men had been making and using guns long before Cartier and Cabot set foot on the land that is now Canada. Even this essential preamble to our story is well illuminated by replicas and displays in the Museum.

From the days of the earliest explorers to the Korean War, for such is the scope of this story, the guns of Canada have been greatly influenced by the French, the British, and lately the Americans. Our guns were nearly always designed abroad and, until the present century, were usually manufactured abroad. It follows that, if we are to preserve a reasonable balance in our account, we must give due recognition to these roots and origins as we encounter them. This I have endeavoured to do.

During the course of a career that focused largely on ballistics, which is the science of gunnery, I have become deeply indebted for information on the subject not only to many colleagues—British, Canadian and Allied—with whom it has been my privilege to serve over the years, but also to innumerable books and publications. A brief list of acknowledgements could hardly avoid being woefully incomplete. The same problem arises in any attempt to suggest sources interested readers might turn to for further information; for every one I might propose there exist many others of comparable value. This being said, I have made a few suggestions, which readers will find in the bibliography on page 109.

The production of this little book is due, in large part, to the initiative, advice and assistance of many of my friends at the Canadian War Museum, in particular to Lee Murray, John Swettenham and Fred Gaffen. Its final form owes much to Viviane Appleton and her colleagues in the Publishing Division of the National Museums of Canada. Louise L. Trahan supervised the French edition, and Jean Pariseau, Senior Historian, Department of National Defence, generously acted as consultant.

I am especially grateful to General E.M.D. Leslie, himself a gunner, who kindly read the text and made many helpful comments.

L.W.C.S.B.
Ottawa, March 1979

1 Richard Jack, *The Taking of Vimy Ridge, Easter Monday, 1917*, oil on canvas, c. 1917–21 (Coll.: Canadian War Museum)

Prologue

In the snowy pre-dawn light of the last day of the year 1775, two columns of American infantry were advancing on the city of Quebec. Montreal had already surrendered and the American rebels saw Canada almost within their grasp. Before the day was out, that dream was to be shattered and Canada given the chance to forge a destiny of her own. The salvation of the young country on that critical day was due in part to the determination of Sir Guy Carleton, in part to the resoluteness of the little garrison of British regulars and French-Canadian militiamen and, no less importantly, to a few assorted pieces of artillery. Some well-aimed rounds of canister- and grape-shot drove one column into retreat and mortally wounded Richard Montgomery, the commanding general of the invading forces. A few hours later, the shaken remnants of the second column eventually capitulated rather than face the fire of a British field gun being unlimbered for action in the narrow streets of Lower Town.

The nation that was given a chance to live on that blustery day in 1775 came of age in another snowstorm almost a century and a half later. Again, victory was achieved by sound leadership, brave troops, and the guns. This time the scene was the slopes of Vimy Ridge, the general was Byng, the soldiers were the Canadian Corps. Their capture of the strategic ridge and an eventual advance of nearly five miles through the strongly fortified German positions were due, in no small part, to a radically new programme of artillery support devised by a young soldier-scientist named Andrew McNaughton.

Artillery, long known as the final arbiter of kings, has played a role in determining Canada's history on many occasions. Its first recorded use in this country was the day in 1534 when Jacques Cartier fired two ship's-cannon to repulse the canoes of Indian warriors in the Baie des Chaleurs. But guns had been speaking their noisy message for more than two hundred years before Cartier erected his cross on the Gaspé coast, and the various "engines of war", to which they were but the technological successors, had played a part in the rise and fall of empires for two thousand years.

The Final Arbiter of Kings
The Prehistory of the Gun

1

3 Catapult

Sticks and Stones

Long before the days of recorded history, man doubtless strove to increase the range and effectiveness of such means as he had of defeating his adversaries. He used clubs and he threw rocks. Eventually he learned to hurl spears and, in due course, to make bows and arrows. Always he was seeking to use the technical knowledge available to him to strike down his enemy with greater certainty and at a greater distance.

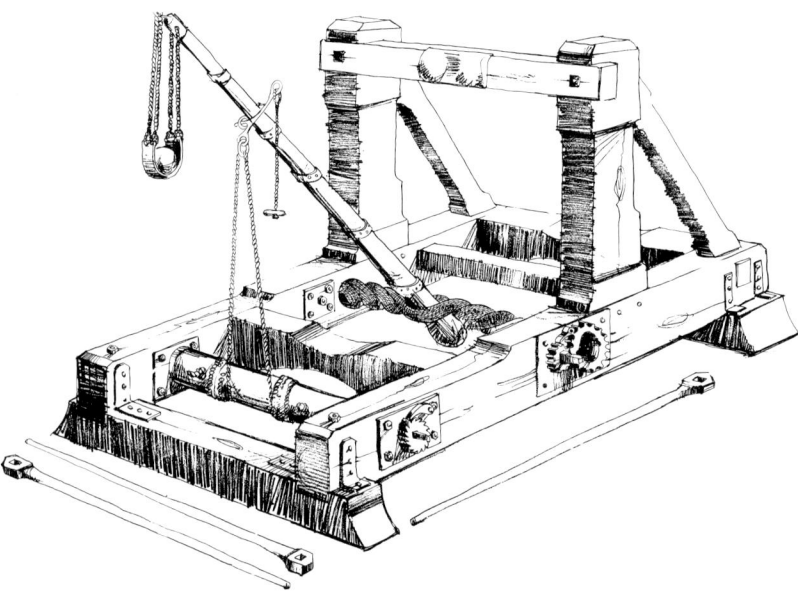

The bow has been known for at least five thousand years, and had been developed to a very effective state when it formed the assault weapon of the infantry of the Assyrian Empire a thousand years before Christ. The bowmen were soon joined by the slingmen, whose simple launcher, as Goliath found to his cost, significantly improved the effectiveness of the hand-thrown stone. Another engine of war regularly employed by the Assyrians was the great battering ram they pounded the walls and gates of enemy cities with.

The last five centuries of the pre-Christian era saw the advent of some of the more obvious ancestors of modern artillery —the many variations on the basic theme of the catapult. Invented by the Phoenicians, developed by the Greeks and by Alexander the Great, and brought close to the peak of their performance by the Romans, catapults varied considerably in size, but all of them launched their projectiles with the aid of energy stored in twisted skeins of animal hide and sinew or, in a famous instance, hair of the women of Carthage. The ballista and the catapult were the siege and field artillery of their day. The missiles they launched varied from arrows weighing half a pound, lethal at 400 yards, to large stones weighing 50 or even 90 pounds, such as those Alexander the Great battered the walls of Tyre with in 332 B.C. When the defenders of a besieged town proved to be particularly obstinate, the ammunition could be changed to pots of burning sulphur and to decomposing animal carcasses—surely the lineal predecessors of the twentieth-century chemical shell.

2 (p. 14) Melchior Feselen, *The Siege of Alesia* (detail), oil on canvas, 1533 (Coll.: Alte Pinakothek, Munich)
  Although this work is intended to depict the battle in which Julius Caesar defeated Vercingetorix in 52 B.C., the painter has treated the event in terms of the warfare of the early sixteenth century. This detail of the painting shows sixteenth-century cannon and mortars being fired from behind a specially constructed entrenchment.

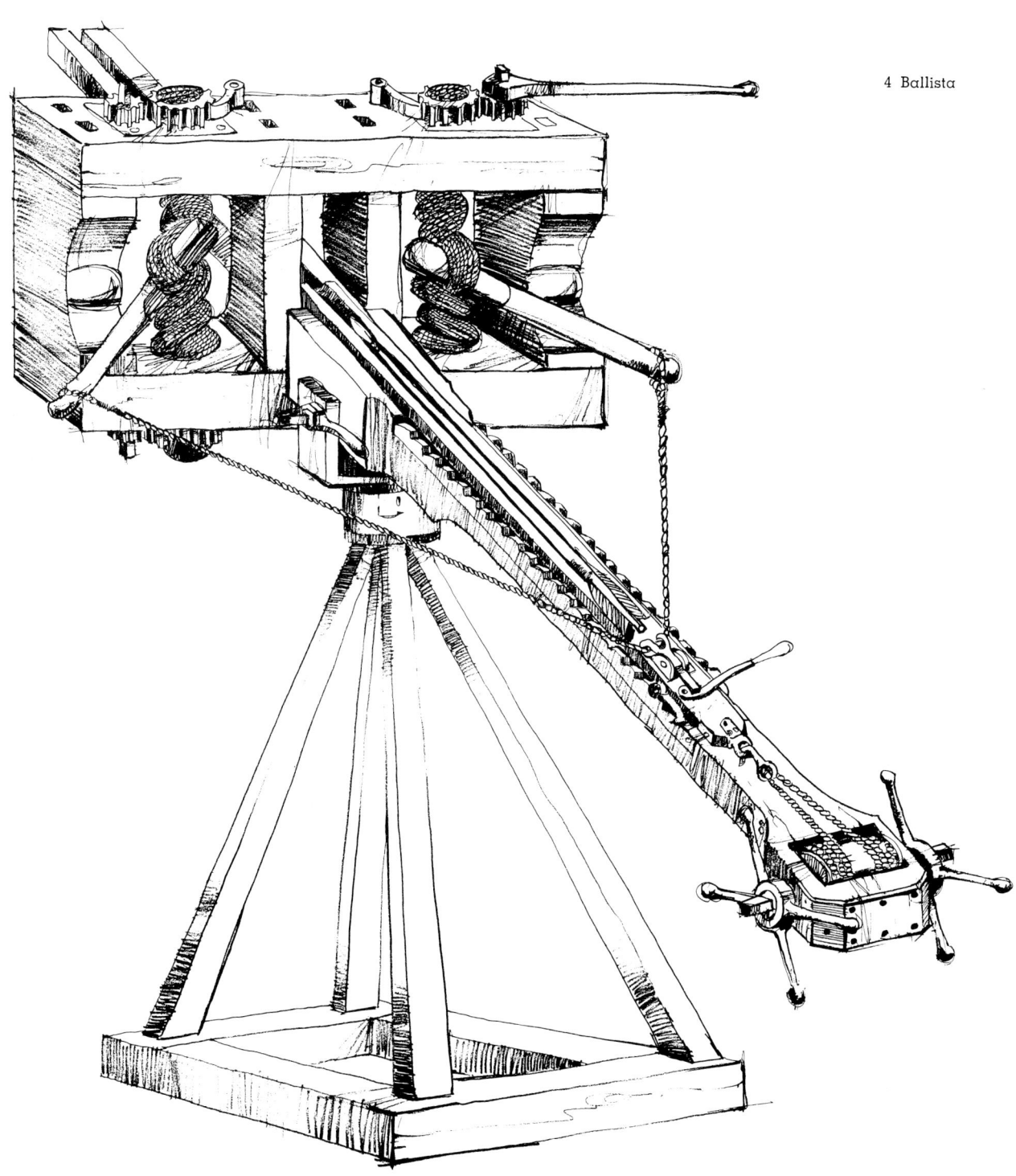

4 Ballista

5 Trebuchet

The catapult family of weapons had an active service life of some two thousand years. A ballista was used very successfully by the British garrison during the siege of Gibraltar in 1780 to drive a party of Spanish soldiers out of a position that none of the fortress guns could reach.

The Middle Ages brought both further development of the ballista and the invention of the last of the great throwing engines, the trebuchet. Unlike the catapult, which employed torsion as the energy source, the trebuchet was powered by massive weights, sometimes of up to 10 tons, that swung the missile launching arm.

"The Devil's Invention"

Just when guns, in any modern sense of the word, first appeared is still the subject of a good deal of debate among military historians. Myths and legends are often more in evidence than facts. One tradition credits an English alchemist and friar named Roger Bacon with the invention of gunpowder, and he was certainly the first to record a surviving formula. However, a case can also be made for the Chinese, Hindus, Greeks, Arabs and Germans. The discovery probably took place no later than the mid-thirteenth century, which antedates any meaningful evidence of the existence of guns by many decades. Gunpowder may have been used in rockets as early as the tenth century, but the first man to make a gun utilizing gunpowder as a propellant is said to have been Berthold Schwarz, a German monk, in 1313. There are some historians, however, who doubt whether the good Berthold ever had other than a legendary existence. Wherever the truth lies, there seems little doubt that the earliest guns were vase-shaped objects loaded with gunpowder, which fired a type of iron dart that had been sealed in the neck with leather binding; the powder was ignited by thrusting a hot wire into a touch-hole. The basic principles of such a *pot-de-fer*, as the French knew it, or *vasi*, as the Italians called it, are well illustrated in a manuscript dated 1326; they remained the essential characteristics of most guns for the next five hundred years.

Edward III probably used guns of some sort in Scotland in 1327. Again, in 1346 at Crécy, the English army had a few bombards, whose main contribution seems to have been to frighten the horses of the French knights.

Even the origins of the words *gun* and *artillery* are shrouded in the mists of antiquity. One fascinating suggestion, which is no more unlikely than many others, is that *gun* had its origin in an affectionate diminutive of a Norman woman's name—Gunnhilda—that had been given to some very early piece of ordnance. There certainly was a Mons Meg in 1483 and a Big Bertha in the First World War; why not a Gunnhilda in the fourteenth century?
As for the word *artillery*, it may well have come from *artilliators*, originally meaning the makers of bows and engines of war for the English kings and later, reflecting the winds of change, the makers of guns.

Siege Warfare

The primitive guns of the fourteenth century probably posed almost as great a threat to the gunners as they did to the enemy; and they clearly had little effect on the conduct of war. In the next century, however, things started to change quite radically. Guns were built that could throw missiles of a weight comparable to those launched by the catapults, which until then had been the essential weapons of siege warfare. Records of the time indicate that the arsenals of Europe contained a mixture of guns and the ancient engines. In 1414 Henry V granted a warrant to one Nicholas Merbury, creating him "Master of the works of our engines, guns and other ordnance of war". It was in the first half of the fifteenth century that the gun began to change the course of military history by eliminating the near invulnerability of the great castles and fortress cities. In 1405 the Duke of Northumberland's previously impregnable Warkworth Castle surrendered after receiving only seven projectiles from Henry IV's siege gun. Ten years later Henry V pounded down the walls of Harfleur with his ten great cannon, known as the King's Daughters. As the Hundred

6 *Pot-de-fer;* replica (Coll.: Canadian War Museum)

7 Mohammed's great gun
(Coll.: Tower of London)

Years' War came to an end and Charles VII of France saw the English occupation of his country reduced to little more than a foothold at Calais, his appreciation should have been directed as much to Jacques Coeur and the Bureau brothers, the first great French artillery experts, as to Joan of Arc. Rouen, Bayonne and Bordeaux may have fallen, as has been claimed, before the resurgence of French patriotism; in practical terms they fell under the pulverizing blows of the great French bombards.

Some of the siege guns of this period were of enormous size, particularly in light of the existing means of transport. The bombard Dulle Griete (Mad Meg), which was built at Ghent in 1430 and has survived, weighs 15 tons and fired a stone shot 25 inches in diameter. Mons Meg, which was made thirty years later (and can still be seen at Edinburgh Castle), fired a 330-pound granite ball a distance of some 3,000 yards. One of the most fantastic of them all was Mohammed's great gun, now at the Tower of London, whose 25-inch shot was used to considerable effect at the siege of Constantinople in 1453. The movement of this great weapon was facilitated by its having been made in two pieces, which could be screwed together. Even so, more than one hundred oxen and two hundred men were required to move it, and it took two months for them to cover 150 miles.

Mohammed's great gun was made of cast bronze, but the typical siege gun of the period was built up from long iron bars assembled around a wooden core. The bars were heated red-hot, and were beaten together until they formed a crude welded tube. Further strength was supplied by iron rings, which while white-hot were placed over the tube and contracted around it as they cooled. What remained of the wooden core was then bored away. The gun at this stage of its manufacture was a simple tube, open at both ends and resembling in its construction a barrel—the name that has been applied to gun tubes ever since. Devising a method of closing the breech end so that the gun could be fired strained the technical abilities of the early gun-makers to the limit. The usual solution was to have some sort of device that not only closed off the end of the gun, but often held the powder charge as well, as was usual with the peterara; a wedge kept the device in place. With larger guns, the closing device was held by a wedge driven between it and the great wooden baulk against which the gun usually rested. One of the most famous figures to suffer the effects of an ill-fitted breech wedge was James II of Scotland, whose "thigh bone was done in two" at the siege of Roxburgh Castle in 1460. The gun was normally strapped to its wooden base or cradle, and sometimes a primitive wooden shield was placed above it to protect the gunners from the arrows and other missiles of the garrison under siege.

8 Peterara; replica (Coll.: Canadian War Museum)

Guns Take to the Field

The great bombards of the first half of the fifteenth century, having vanquished the castles and radically changed one of the traditional aspects of warfare in the Middle Ages, were supplemented by smaller guns, which brought about further changes. The next fifty years were to see the first victories of artillery over the two forces that had dominated many of the battlefields of Europe for more than a hundred and fifty years—the Swiss pikemen and the English bowmen.

The immobility and slow firing rate of the great bombards had limited their role to the attack of fixed fortifications; they played little if any part in more mobile warfare. The smaller guns, in their earliest versions, while more readily transportable, produced very little in the way of effective firepower. The guns that Edward III took to Scotland in 1327 do not appear to have had any significant effect on the morale of the Highlanders; and at Crécy the chivalry of France suffered immeasurably more from the grey-goose-fletched arrows set flying by the longbows of the yeomen of England than they did from Edward's three horse-frightening cannon. A hundred years later the picture was beginning to change. In 1450, two field guns were the key to the success of French arms at the Battle of Formigny. For the first time, the fire of these artillery pieces achieved the tactical objective that the mounted knights alone had been unable to accomplish in the past: it broke the solid defensive line of English archers and men-at-arms, opening the way for a major French victory. And so it was at Marignano (Corsica) in 1515, when a few cannon again turned the tide of battle and ended the long supremacy of the 18-foot ash pike, tipped with a 10-inch head of steel and held by superbly disciplined Swiss soldiers to form a bristling wall, impenetrable to both horse and man. The pikemen, having formed a defensive "hedgehog" against attacks by the French cavalry, created an ideal target for the guns, and for the first time they were forced to leave the field.

As if in some symbolic salute, at both Formigny and Marignano, the new weapon of artillery gave the classical armoured horsemen the opportunity to overcome the bowmen and pikemen that had so often proved their undoing in the past. These hours of glory, however, proved to be but the last burst of sunshine before the final twilight. By the end of the sixteenth century their temporary ally, gunpowder, had been turned upon them, virtually banishing fully armoured cavalry from the field of battle.

The guns that sounded the knell of the pikemen and the bowmen were probably cast in either brass or iron. They were probably fired off two-wheeled carriages, stabilized in some cases by two wooden struts, which were lowered to the ground in action. The struts might well have served as the base of shafts to enable horses to pull the guns when they had to be moved. For use in the field, the original method of anchoring the gun to an immobile wooden beam, called a *tiller,* had largely given way to the adoption of wheeled carriages of various sorts. Sometimes these were "carts of war", like those the barons of Scotland had to produce for their king in 1456; or they may have been as elaborate as those prototypes of armoured fighting vehicles which General Zizka, the Hussite leader, belaboured his German opponents with in the 1520s. An illustration of cannon being brought into action at the Battle of Marignano shows guns and carriages that would not have appeared outlandish to the gunners of Waterloo, three hundred years later. Indeed, the ghost of the fifteenth-century Nicholas Merbury would have felt reasonably at home wandering on All-Hallows-Eve through the gun lines of Marlborough's or Wellington's armies.

The Art and Craft of Gun-Making

The art of casting guns in brass began to develop early in Europe. Short-barrelled brass mortars had been made by the craftsmen of Florence as early as 1326, and casting a *pot-de-fer* would not have seemed a particularly difficult task to an experienced bell-founder. Early in the fifteenth century, the European gun-founders were carrying on a thriving export trade. James I of Scotland imported what was described as "a monstrous brass gun", but within a few years traditional sagacity led the Scotch Parliament to agree that for both strategic and economic reasons a home-based industry should be developed.

9 Early field gun

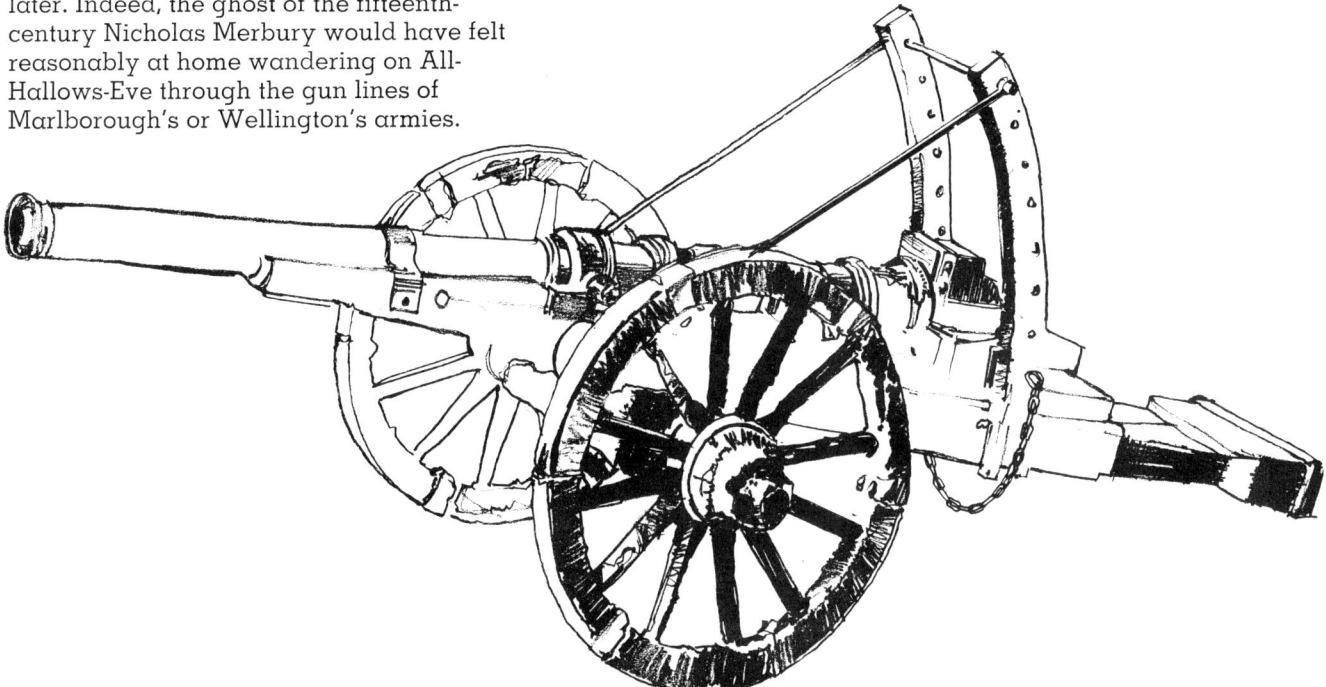

10 Small bronze cannon barrel cast by Mathew Bagley, c. 1700 (Coll.: Canadian War Museum)

Well before the century was over, the gun-founders of Scotland were casting weapons in a wide range of sizes and establishing a tradition in this difficult art that would lead, some three hundred years later, to the production by the Carron Iron Works of the famous carronades, the "smashers", which were mounted on more than four hundred ships of the Royal Navy during the Napoleonic Wars.

Brass and bronze (the latter sometimes known as gunmetal) were used in early gun production. The actual choice in any particular instance was governed by knowledge, custom and the nature of the weapon being cast. *Brass* is the name applied to alloys of copper and zinc in various proportions. Copper is the major constituent, and the percentages of zinc range from two to thirty-six depending on the characteristics that are required in the alloy, which increases in strength and hardness as more zinc is added. Small quantities of lead and tin were sometimes included to facilitate casting. *Bronze* is an alloy of copper and tin (when the percentages of the two metals are in the order of ninety to ten respectively, the material is known as gunmetal). These two basic alloys, with various modifications, were used for gun-casting from the fourteenth century until well into the nineteenth, when they were finally superseded by iron and steel.

One of the great advantages of casting a gun, as opposed to building it up from wrought-iron bars, was that it would allow formation of a barrel open only at one end; the problem of effectively sealing the breech was thereby solved. Some of the earlier cast guns were made for breech-loading but, by and large, the cast gun was a muzzle-loader. The art of the gun-founders borrowed much from that of their fellow craftsmen, the bell-founders. The molten metal was poured between two moulds: the inner one, usually made of clay, governed the internal shape and dimensions of the barrel, and an outer mould of clay or sand controlled the external. Gun-casting was not only a rather dangerous occupation (as late as 1716 Mathew Bagley, a leading English founder, and twenty of his men were killed by an explosion when brass was being poured into what was presumably a damp mould), but the quality of the end product was always unpredictable. It is not surprising that proof-testing of at least some new guns was carried out in England as early as 1456.

The obvious alternative to brass and bronze for gun-casting was iron, but, while much cheaper, it had a number of disadvantages. In particular, the casting process was more difficult, and iron was more brittle than were the copper alloys. A defect in the barrel was likely to result in a devastating explosion without the warning bulge that usually occurred in a brass gun under similar stress. Nevertheless, the economics of the case were heavily on the side of cast iron, and Henry VIII decided to follow the lead that had already been established on the Continent. The first cast-iron gun to be manufactured in England was produced in Sussex in 1543. The Weald of Kent and Sussex, with readily available supplies of both charcoal and iron ore, and water power to blow the bellows of the newly imported blast furnaces, remained the centre of the industry for many years. Even today the observant traveller can see traces of the Wealden iron works, which helped to arm the little ships with which Howard, Drake and Hawkins outranged the great galleons of the Spanish Armada and harried them to their destruction in 1588.

"A Black Powder That Kills with Much Noise"

Whether the guns were made of brass or bronze, cast iron or wrought iron, they all used gunpowder as their propellant; and if the design of guns advanced but slowly, the art of gunpowder manufacture developed at an even statelier pace. In the early days, the finely mixed "serpentine", or mealed powder, was liable to separate into its three components of sulphur, saltpetre and charcoal, with the denser material falling to the bottom when it was subjected to vibration during travel. For this reason it was not uncommon for the components to be mixed at, or very near, the scene of action. In addition, the loading of the dense powder into the gun called for a great deal of experience. Packed either too tightly or too loosely, it failed to burn properly. So important was this task of loading that the expert whose responsibility it was began to be known by the always respected name of Master Gunner.

Early in the fifteenth century the technique for "corning" powder was discovered, in which an evaporation process locked the ingredients into grains, whose size could be varied to meet the needs of different guns. Corned powder burned more regularly, cleanly and powerfully than serpentine; because of the last characteristic, it was not widely used for almost a hundred years, until guns became strong enough to handle it with reasonable safety. The effects of corning together with gradual increases in the proportion of saltpetre in the powder (from Bacon's forty-one per cent up to about seventy-five per cent) enabled the size of gunpowder charges to be reduced from rough equality with the weight of the shot in the fourteenth century to about half that of the projectile in the eighteenth century.

11 Double ignition of mortar and fuse

Projectiles Plain and Fancy

The dart-like missile fired from the *pot-de-fer* did not become the typical ammunition of the earliest gunners. Solid round shot provided the most effective means of battering the walls of fortresses, and these balls began to appear in the diameters needed to fit the many types of guns that were being produced. Stone shot, often of granite, was most commonly used, as the more effective iron shot was more expensive. Other than against the individual man standing right in the line of fire, this type of shot was clearly ineffective in what today would be called an anti-personnel role. The Venetians appreciated this problem as early as 1376, when they found an answer in a projectile made by fitting together two hemispherical bronze forms, which they filled with gunpowder and fired from short-barrelled mortars. This "shell" probably exploded (amongst either friend or foe) with the aid of a simple fuse the gunner ignited just before he fired the gun. It is doubtful that this type of projectile played any significant role before the sixteenth century, but there is evidence that it was used with considerable effect at the siege of Bergen-op-Zoom in 1588. By this time, shells were usually made of iron.

26

The rate of fire of the guns of this early period was so slow that there was often time for only one round to be fired at advancing enemy troops before they reached the gun position. It was not long before various devices were tried to increase the number of hits from this one precious round. Case shot, or "canister", was used at Constantinople in 1453. It consisted of small stones or, later, metal balls that were loaded in a container (or canister) and fired with potentially devastating effect into massed troops at short range. The range of the sub-projectiles was eventually increased and their scatter controlled by packing them in layers within a simple bag or framework. A rough similarity in form between the resultant ammunition and a bunch of grapes was responsible for the name it was known by for several centuries—grapeshot.

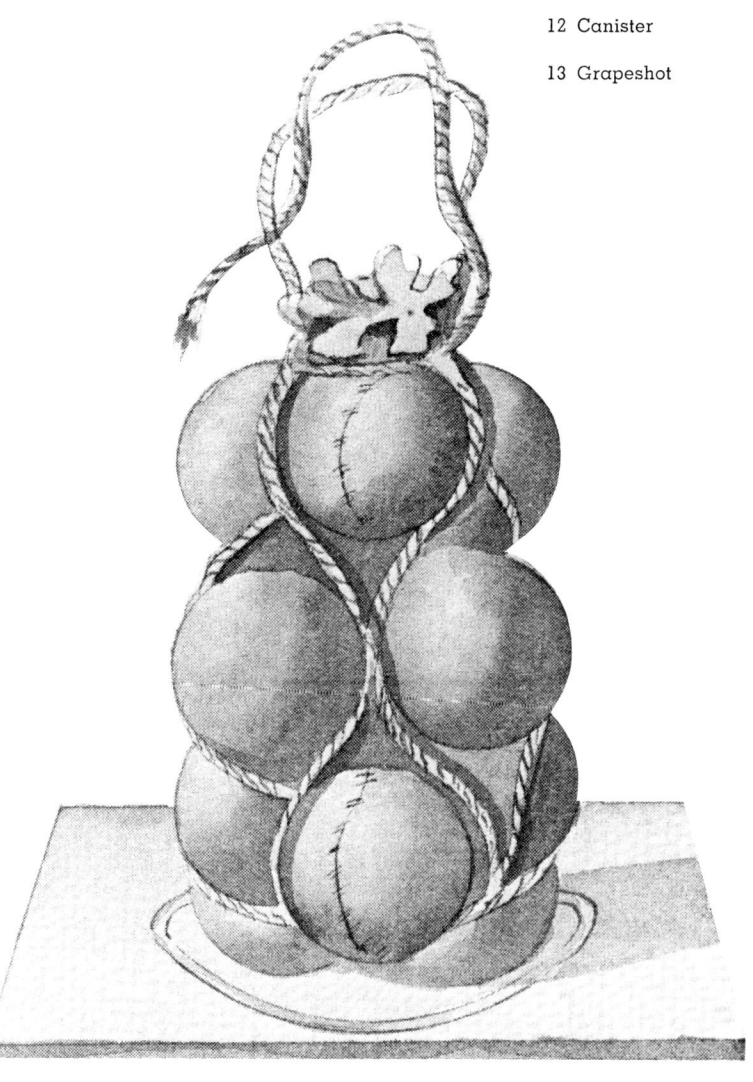

12 Canister

13 Grapeshot

The Struggle for Canada:
Gunnery in the Age of Reason

2

14 (p. 28) *A View of the Taking of Quebec, 13 September 1759* (detail), engraving published 1 November 1797 by Laurie and Whittle (Coll.: Public Archives of Canada)

In this unknown artist's conception of the Battle of the Plains of Abraham, British soldiers can be seen dragging a 6-pounder up the cliff.

The Swamps and Forests of Canada

Difficult as it was to move the massive cast-iron and brass guns of the time over the indifferent roads of seventeenth-century Europe, it was virtually impossible to move them through the swamps and forests of Canada. Thus it was that only the lightest of ordnance was to be found outside the confines of established forts, such as Quebec and Port Royal. A few attempts were made to provide the French troops with artillery support during their campaigns against the Indians, but the almost insurmountable problems of land transportation usually cancelled out any tactical advantage the guns might have provided. Frontenac discovered this to his cost during the campaign against the Onondaga in 1696, when, having conveyed an assortment of cannon, mortars and rockets in his bateaux, he had to unload them and then advance with them through dense woods. Even the guns of the forts were few and small in these early days. They were the naval guns of the period, mounted on wooden carriages. When David Kirke captured Quebec in 1629, the French had fewer than a dozen small guns and mortars available to defend the town.

Coastal Defence and Siege Warfare

As the eighteenth century approached, however, the artillery defences of the fortresses and the siege weapons of the forces that attacked them began to play a far more significant role in Canada's history. When Sir William Phips arrived on the St. Lawrence below Quebec in October 1690, he was given a much more depressing reception than that which Kirke's expedition of 1629 had received. Instead of finding a few small guns—no match for the armament of the invading fleet—Phips's ships were bombarded by batteries of 18- and 24- pounders, which effectively covered the water approaches to the city. Well might Frontenac assure Phips's representative that he would answer the British general only by the mouths of his cannon. He soon showed that he was in an excellent position to do so. The guns of the fleet, unable to cause significant damage to either the defences of Quebec or the morale of its citizens, did little more than waste the ammunition that might have been more usefully employed in support of the abortive landing that preceded Phips's final withdrawal to Boston.

The big guns played an even more important part in the two sieges of the great fortress of Louisbourg, which took place in 1745 and 1758. The War of the Austrian Succession gave the New Englanders their first opportunity to try the true strength of the allegedly impregnable fortress that their French rivals had spent more than twenty-five years building. Realizing that the thirty guns and four mortars they were able to bring with them would be unable to breach the walls of Louisbourg, the attackers planned to capture siege guns from the enemy and brought along only a supply of cannonballs of the appropriate size. The scheme was carried out without a hitch, and an assault party occupied an outlying battery with very little opposition.

15 Émile and Adolphe Rouargue, *Défense de Québec par M. de Frontenac, 1690*, engraving, 1846. (Coll.: Public Archives of Canada)
Frontenac's cannon engage the English ships during Phips's attack on Quebec.

16 Mortar from the fortress of Louisbourg (Coll.: Canadian War Museum)

This prize provided them not only with heavy guns but also with the gunpowder to fire them. Within seven weeks, the "Dunkirk of New France" had been pounded into surrender. Louisbourg having been restored to its original owners by the Treaty of Aix-la-Chapelle, the British forces faced the task of recapturing it as soon as the Seven Years' War broke out. This time they brought their own siege artillery—eighty-eight guns, six howitzers, and fifty-two mortars of assorted calibres. Surrender came within thirty-eight days, but at the cost of twice as much ammunition as had been expended in the bombardment thirteen years earlier.

When Wolfe moved on from Louisbourg to Quebec he took some powerful artillery units with him; but they played little part in the final attack, which was essentially an infantry battle. The French were short of both powder and gunners, though they deployed at least four field guns. There were only two British 6-pounder guns in action on the Plains of Abraham on 13 September 1759. Nevertheless, a gunner's tradition has it that it was a round of grapeshot from one of these pieces that inflicted the wound Montcalm eventually died from. The actual surrender of Quebec on September 17 was undoubtedly hastened by the British force's deployment of siege guns on the Plains of Abraham with the obvious intent of bombarding the city. The guns at least contributed to the final victory by their mere presence. It was a simple illustration of the doctrine of power in being.

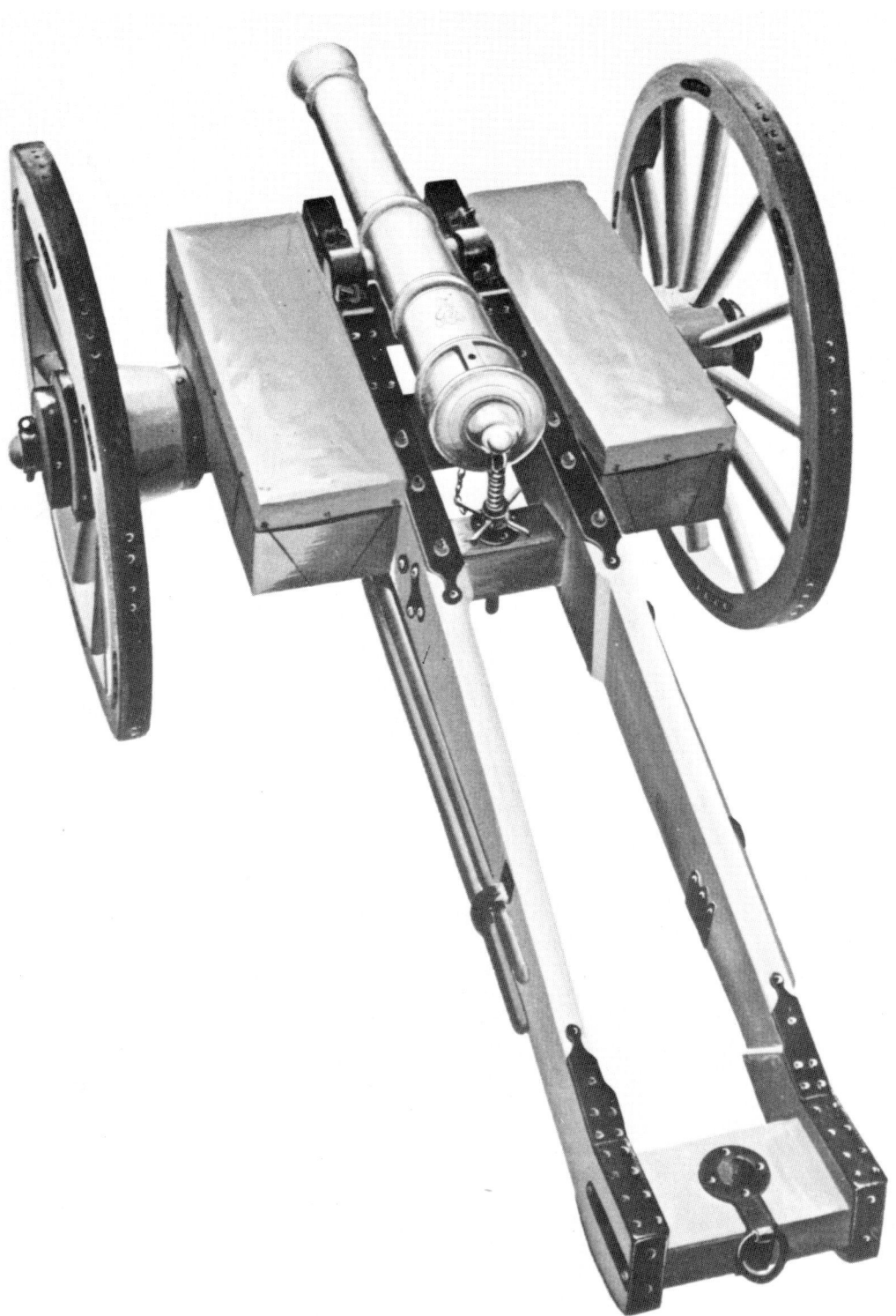

17 A 6-pounder used by Wolfe's troops at Quebec. The axle was widened and fitted with ammunition boxes for service in Canada.

A King Effects a Revolution

In the century or so that preceded the fall of New France, artillery had undergone several notable developments. The modern concept of the field gun had its origin with King Gustavus Adolphus of Sweden, who encouraged the production of guns light enough to travel with the infantry. He also rationalized the nomenclatures and calibres of his artillery, which he limited to 24-, 12-, 6- and 4-pounders. The British system, in contrast, recognized at least sixteen models, ranging from the Cannon Royal (which weighed 4.5 tons and fired a 70-pound shot) through basilisks, culverins, sakers, falcons and many other creatures both real and mythical, down to the little robinet, which weighed 300 pounds and consumed three-quarters of a pound of powder every time it fired its half-pound shot.

18 Early examples of fixed ammunition

The Swedish king was also an early advocate of fixed ammunition. His 4-pounders had their powder charges already weighed out in flannel bags, and these were supplied, with the shot, in wooden boxes. The result was a rate of fire faster than that of a musket, something quite beyond the capacity of a gun whose powder for every round had to be loaded loose by means of an iron ladle.

The seventeenth century also saw an increasing use of the portfire to ignite the charge. This was a piece of quickmatch, clamped in a long holder, that was lit from a constantly glowing slowmatch just before the firing of each round; and as promptly extinguished by means of a clipper until the next round was loaded. Later in the century the French invented the limber, consisting originally of two wheels and an axle, which could be coupled on the trail of a gun to transport it. (The trail is the lower end of a gun carriage, whose purpose is to stabilize the gun.) The adoption of the limber, to which was soon added a box to carry ammunition, further increased the mobility of field equipments. At about the same time, the elevating screw was gaining popularity as a substitute for the wedge, or quoin, which nevertheless remained in use as a means of adjusting the elevation of some heavier guns for a hundred years more.

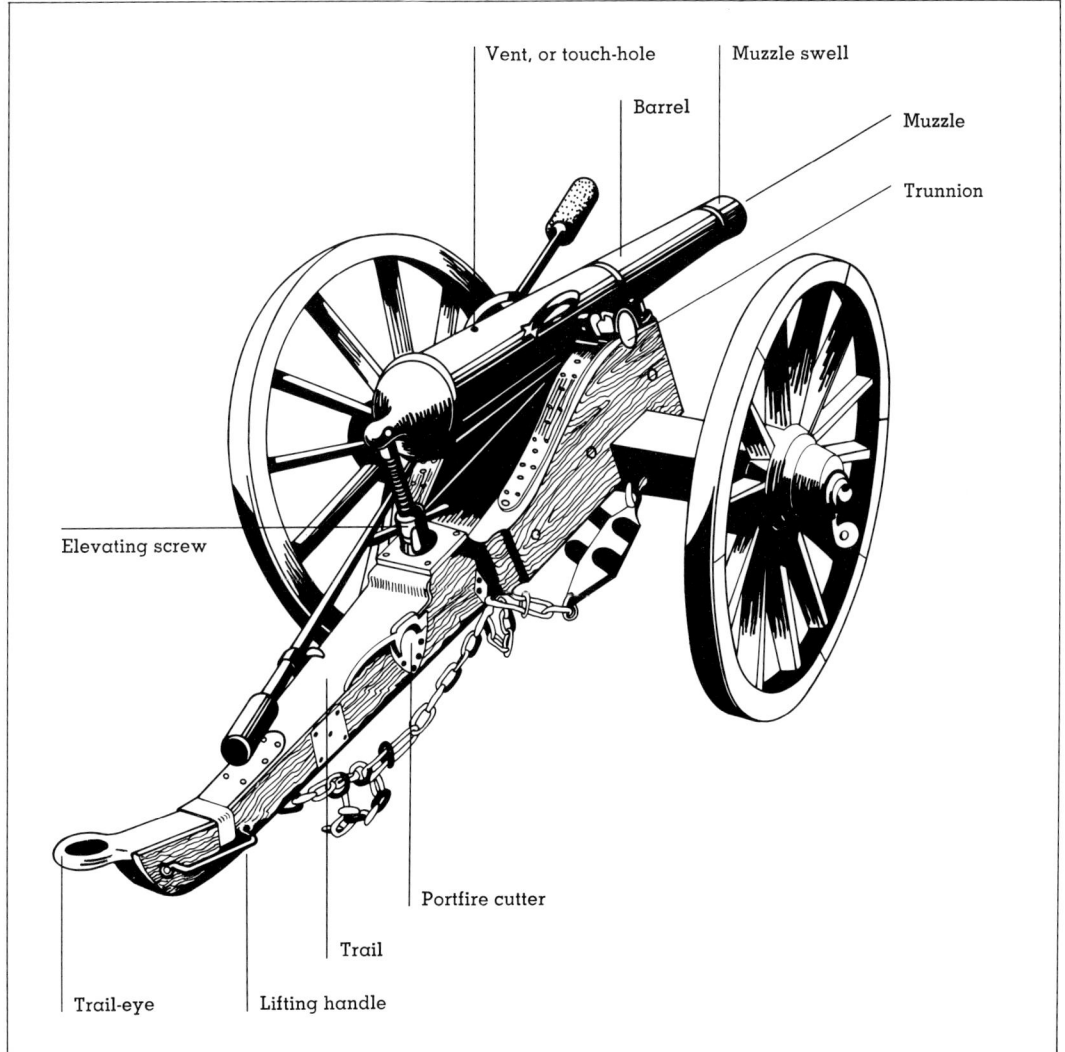

19 An eighteenth-century bronze field gun

20. Royal mortar, c. 1807
(Coll.: Tower of London,
on extended loan to the
Canadian War Museum)

Mortars and howitzers were now appearing in an ever increasing variety of calibres, and, as we have seen, they played their various parts in actions in Canada. Mortars were then essentially short-barrelled weapons that fired bombs filled with gunpowder. The elevation of the piece was often fixed at 45 degrees, and range was controlled by adjusting the weight of the powder charge. They were short-range weapons that subjected their often temperamental ammunition to a minimum shock of discharge. The principle of the howitzer, which traces its name back to the Bohemian word *houfnice*, or catapult, was similar to that of the mortar, but it was a more powerful piece and its range could be adjusted by means of elevation as well as by powder charge. The plunging fire of both these weapons, coming down on the far side of defensive walls, was often used in attacking fortified positions.

Advances in weapon design went hand in hand with tactical developments. The availability of 6-pounder field guns of reasonable mobility together with the Duke of Marlborough's skill in utilizing their capabilities at critical moments were probably responsible for his victory at the Battle of Blenheim in 1704. During the Seven Years' War, some fifty years later, 6-pounder "battalion guns" were an integral part of the support available to the infantry. A few weeks before Wolfe gained immortality on the Plains of Abraham, with only the minimum of assistance from his guns, a landmark in the history of British artillery had been established on the other side of the Atlantic. The outcome of the Battle of Minden (Germany) was decided by ten 12-pounder field guns, which came to the aid of the battered infantry and turned what might well have been a final victorious French cavalry charge into a rout.

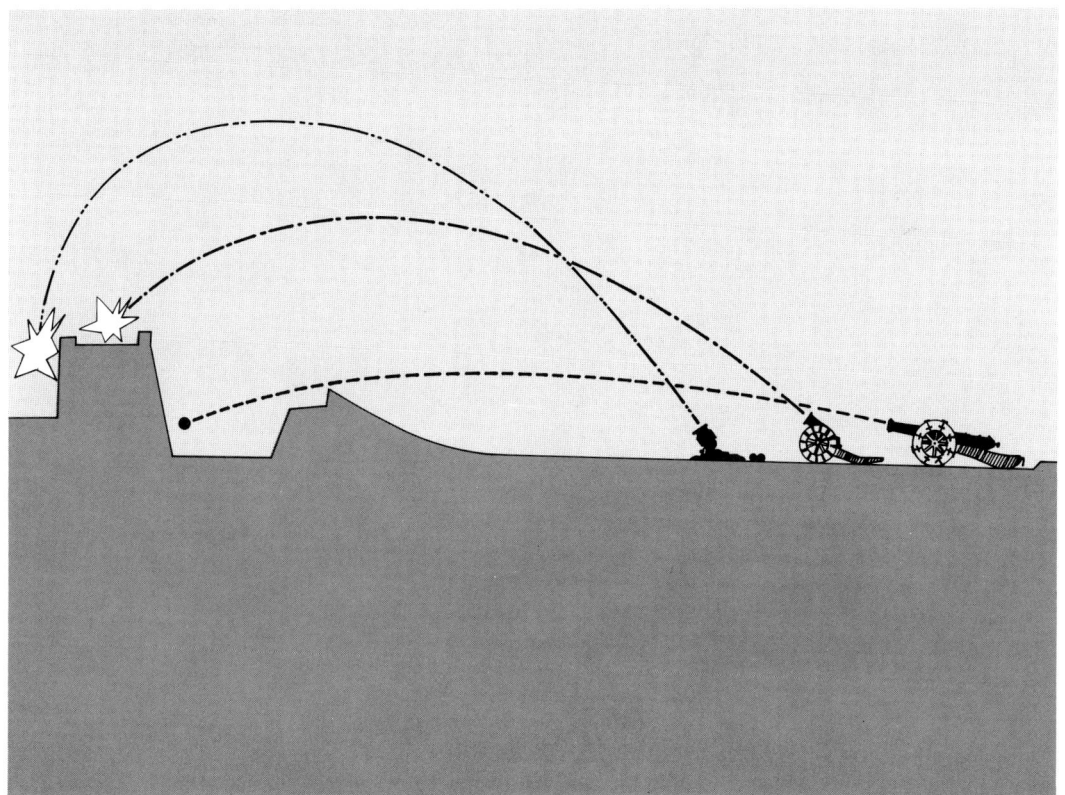

21 The trajectories of a mortar, howitzer and cannon *(left to right)*

22 A 12-pounder field gun of Marlborough's period; replica (Coll.: Rotunda Museum, Woolwich, England)

Ballistics, the Science of Gunnery

Ballistics, the science of gunnery, was for all practical purposes founded in the eighteenth century. It is true that as early as 1578 attempts had been made to measure the strength of gunpowder by firing samples in a little mortar fitted with a heavy hinged lid and observing the lid's angle of rise. In the next century, firing tests were carried out in several European countries to determine the relationships between the weight of the powder charge, the elevation of the gun, and the range achieved. While experiments of this nature doubtless provided a good deal of useful information, they can hardly be seen as forming the basis of a scientifc study of all the factors governing the motion of the projectile in the gun, in flight, and at the target. In other words, the meaningful study of internal, external and terminal ballistics had yet to begin. Among other characteristics, it is generally agreed that a science must offer scope for the making of measurements and that it must have at least an underpinning of theory to relate and explain experimental observations. Gunners had to wait until the eighteenth century before these two basic criteria were achieved.

Many of the essential foundations of modern sciences, such as chemistry and physics, were laid by brilliant individuals, often gifted amateurs by present-day standards, who lived and worked in the eighteenth century. This was the age of Lavoisier and Davy, Cavendish and Priestley, Scheele and Dalton. In the field of ballistics, names such as Robins and Thompson are equally well remembered. Both of these men were pioneers in making the measurements essential to a proper understanding of ballistic processes.

The forces of gravity and of air resistance act on every projectile from the moment that it leaves the muzzle of the gun. Of these forces, air resistance is by far the most complex, and very little was known about it in the eighteenth century. Without a good knowledge of how and why the cannonball or other projectile was slowed down as it moved along its trajectory, it was virtually impossible to calculate its muzzle velocity from the measured range and to relate range and muzzle velocity. Estimates that neglected air resistance were of very limited value. Yet, until 1742, no practical means had been devised for measuring the velocity of a shot in flight. In that year, Benjamin Robins was able to determine the velocity of a musket-ball with the aid of an instrument he called a ballistic pendulum. In essence this consisted of a massive wooden pendulum that swung freely in a stout cage.

When a musket-ball was fired into the free end of the pendulum, the length of the resultant swing could be measured. Once the length and weight of the pendulum and the weight of the ball were known, only a simple calculation was required to determine the velocity with which the shot had struck. By moving the equipment farther away from the muzzle of the musket, Robins was able to record the gradual reduction in velocity as the ball moved along its trajectory. This crude instrument was further refined, and by 1791 Charles Hutton was able to measure the velocity of shot weighing a pound during tests carried out at Woolwich. The Fellows of the Royal Society chose well when they awarded the Copley Gold Medal to Robins in 1747 in recognition of his work. With some justification he entitled the book that contained the results of his research *The New Principles of Gunnery*.

Prior to the eighteenth century, if men knew very little about the theoretical aspects of external ballistics they knew even less about internal ballistics—what actually happened inside a gun when it was fired. As Robins had opened one door through the development of a technique of measurement, so Benjamin Thompson, Count Rumford, opened another. In 1792 he provided a means of making a reasonable assessment of the pressures in the chamber and barrel of a gun as the projectile travelled down the bore. Thompson, like Robins, had to make his measurements indirectly. His main piece of equipment was not unlike a mortar mounted in a perpendicular position, with a piston fitted in its muzzle. Weights were loaded on the piston until it barely moved in response to the firing of a small charge of powder in the mortar. This gave an indication of the pressure in the bore, and from this it became possible to make reasonable estimates of muzzle velocities under various conditions.

It was to be half way through the nineteenth century before an American, General Thomas J. Rodman, invented a method of actually measuring the pressure in the chamber of almost any gun by the indentation of a copper plate. (This can best be explained if the reader will imagine a cylinder fitted with a piston and placed in the chamber of a gun. The gas produced by the explosion of the charge will drive the piston forward. A knife blade on the outer face of the piston is thereby driven into a copper plate, and from the depth of the cut the pressure is determined.) It was even later before Captain Paul-Emile Boulengé of the Belgian artillery invented the electrical chronograph, which measured the time a projectile took to travel a short distance, and hence its actual velocity. In the meanwhile, Robins, the amateur mathematician, and Thompson, the Anglo-American who became a count of the Holy Roman Empire, a British cavalry commander in the American War of Independence and grand chamberlain to the Elector of Bavaria, had provided the initial tools that were essential to the development of ballistics.

23 Artillery of the early eighteenth century

During the eighteenth century, the new science of gunnery also contributed to the increase of scientific knowledge in other areas. In the middle of the century, a team of French Academicians made the first reliable determination of the velocity of sound in air by noting the time between seeing the flashes and hearing the sound of two guns fired thirty kilometres apart. For more than a hundred years, guns continued to be used in ever more refined experiments. As late as 1871 the then Astronomer Royal at Cape Town, South Africa, used a gun and an elaborate series of electrical chronographs to arrive at the velocity of 1,096.6 feet per second, which was accepted as a standard for many years thereafter.

The Right Honourable Board

Throughout much of our story the guns of Canada were influenced, both directly and indirectly, by a body that, in numerous guises and under various titles, has existed for well over five hundred years. The eighteenth century was one of the most influential periods in the history of what was then known as the Right Honourable and Honourable, the Board of His Majesty's Ordnance. The roots of the Board, then a department of state second in importance only to the Treasury itself, can be traced back to 1414, when Nicholas Merbury, whom we have already met, became the first Master of the King's Ordnance. In 1683, Charles II laid upon the Board the responsibility of providing the ships and forts of the realm with the necessary armament. From this authority sprang the Royal Regiment of Artillery and the Royal Engineers and, by devolution, their Canadian counterparts. The executive office of Master General of the Ordnance was held by some of the most famous soldiers of their times, including Sir Philip Sydney; John Churchill, first Duke of Marlborough; and the Duke of Wellington, who was appointed four years after Waterloo. The Master General was not only responsible for the supply of guns and ammunition, but was also Commander in Chief of the Artillery and Engineers, a responsibility he continued to carry until the Crimean War in 1855.

The French Wars of the eighteenth century stirred the imaginative powers of many inventors, and the Board of Ordnance was swamped with proposals for both new weapons and improvements in existing equipment. In 1765 the Board established two committees—the Colonel's Committee and the Field Officer's Committee "to review inventions and ideas and to advise the Surveyer-General [an officer of the Board] which were worthy of his attention". As Brigadier Norman Skentelbery, the historian of the Board, has pointed out: "they were essentially committees of users having no pretensions to advanced scientific or engineering ability".* The military scientist had yet to be officially recognized.

It must be admitted that, over time, some persons who failed to appreciate the merits and value of the Board have pointed to the magnificent coat of arms granted to it during Wellington's term of office. The shield is blazoned with three field guns and three cannonballs—all very appropriate to the motto *Sua tela tonanti* ("His weapons thundering"). The problem was the obvious discrepancy between the calibre of the guns and the diameter of the round shot!

Significant as all these eighteenth-century developments were, the gun itself remained much as it had always been—muzzle-loading, smooth-bored, of brass or iron, and utilizing gunpowder to propel a projectile that was usually a solid iron ball to a range that was usually measured in hundreds of yards. It was to remain so, by and large, until well into the nineteenth century.

---

*Skentelbery, "The Ordnance Board—An Historical Note", Annex A, *Ordnance Board Proceedings* 40, 169. 6 Oct. 1964.

The War of 1812 and After: The Age of Invention

3

24 (p. 44) A. Sherriff Scott, *Climax of the Action at Crysler's Farm, 11 November 1813* (detail of mural at Crysler Farm Battlefield Park, Ont.)

25 Brass 3-pounder cannon, c. 1807, on naval carriage (Coll.: Canadian War Museum)

The Invader Repelled

President Madison, sure in the belief that concentration on the real or imagined failings of some foreigner or other can be relied upon to help a politician to garner badly needed votes, took his country into war with Great Britain in 1812. While his assessment of the reaction of the American voters was accurate enough to secure his re-election, he was very much mistaken in thinking that Canadians would welcome the opportunity to follow his drums out of colonialism and into the welcoming arms of the United States. The guns of both the Canadian militia and the British regulars played varied and useful roles in delivering this message.

As usual, the artillery that was available beyond the limits of the rivers, the lakes and the forts was both small in calibre and few in number. Fortunately for the future of Canada, Isaac Brock was probably the only general of any significant ability on either side of this rather incompetently managed war, and he knew how to get the best advantage out of the few guns at his disposal. Right at the start, his forces seized the initiative and took the American fort on Mackinac Island in a bloodless action, aided by the mere threat of an iron 6-pounder that had been brought by canoe, and much manhandling, to a spot where it commanded the enemy position. Before Detroit surrendered to him, he did fire his few 6-pounders and his 3-pounder "grasshoppers", but his tactical initiatives served to magnify their effect well beyond their reasonable potential.

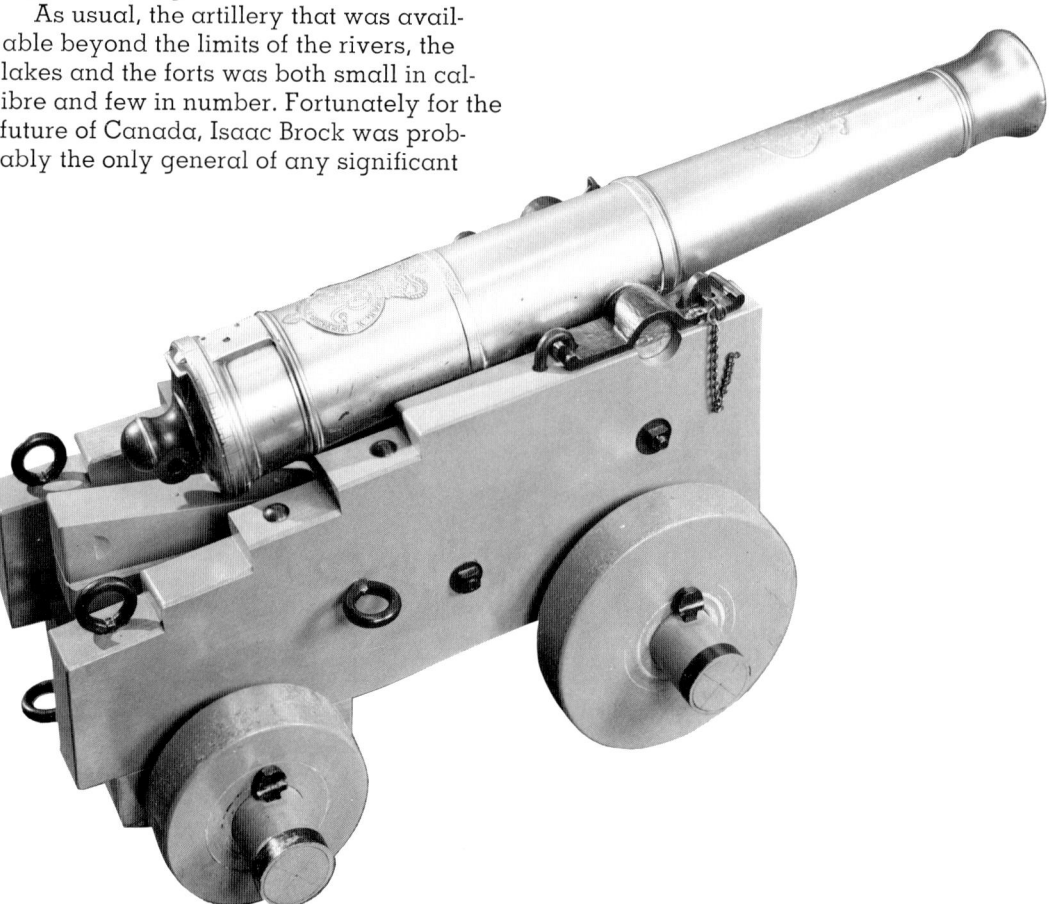

Although the war was to go on for another two years, Queenston Heights on 13 October 1812 can be seen as both a military and a psychological turning-point in the campaign. There Brock made it quite clear that, whatever manifest destiny might claim, Canada was not to be America's for the taking. Once again, the number of Canadian and British guns could be counted on little more than the fingers of one hand. By their skilful deployment, however, Brock (and, after his death in action, his successor) managed to bring fire to bear wherever it was most needed —against the initial American advance, against reinforcements crossing the Niagara River and, in the end, against the rear of the encircled invaders.

Invention in the Field: Shrapnel and Others

In using his few guns to such good effect, Brock was assisted by the availability of a relatively new and quite revolutionary type of ammunition—Henry Shrapnel's "spherical case-shot". Shrapnel's name has provided military jargon with one of its most commonly used (and misused) words, and it is interesting to note that the idea it is associated with was probably developed in Newfoundland.

The basic problem of how to engage troops in the open at a range beyond that of case- or grape-shot was one that had faced gunners since the earliest days. Nowhere was the problem more acutely felt than during the great siege of Gibraltar, which lasted from 1779 to 1783. In gunnery, as in many other human activities, necessity is a spur to invention, and the siege provided the British with many necessities. As a result, the garrison discovered how to design gun carriages that would permit the pieces to be fired at depression (with the barrel pointing down), how to fire red-hot shot as a routine operation, and how to discourage the Spanish troops from working in the open beyond the immediate vicinity of the Rock. To force the Spanish to take cover, an infantry officer suggested that the gunners might try firing the gunpowder-filled shells intended for the short-range 5.5-inch mortars out of their 24-pounder guns, which were of the same calibre. By careful adjustment of the rather primitive fuses, it was found that these shells could be made to burst in flight reasonably close to the enemy. The effect on the Spaniards was such that the officer's bright idea was adopted for regular use.

26 F. Arrowsmith, *Henry Shrapnel*, oil on canvas, 1817 (Coll.: Rotunda Museum, Woolwich, England)

While a bursting iron shell was much more effective against troops in the open than a solid cannonball, it was still far from ideal. Not only was fragmentation uncontrolled as to size but, by being dispersed in all directions, a good deal of its potential effect was wasted. The need was for fragments of an optimum size that could be directed reasonably accurately onto the target. A very promising approach to a workable solution was developed by a young artillery officer named Henry Shrapnel during a tour of garrison duty at St. John's, Newfoundland. His design, which he put forward in 1784, used a relatively thin-walled cast-iron shell filled with lead bullets and a small gunpowder charge just powerful enough to burst the shell but not disperse the bullets, which continued to travel forward in a conical pattern. The fuse that Shrapnel employed to detonate his shell had been in existence for a number of years, and consisted in essence of a wooden tube filled with slow-burning powder and marked on the outside with a series of ridges. Each ridge represented a certain burning time, and the fuse was cut off at such a point that it would explode the shell as close as possible to the optimum point on its trajectory.

While this fuse was a crude device (its timing was often checked against the recitation of the Apostles' Creed), it sufficed, and the resulting round was very effective.

In the nature of things, ingenious inventions by junior officers are rarely seized upon with alacrity by their seniors. So it was with Shrapnel's shell. For some years the inventor experimented with "spherical case-shot" at his own expense. Used in action, the device impressed not only the French troops at the receiving end of the demonstration but also, fortunately, the future Duke of Wellington. He pursuaded the Select Committee of Artillery Officers to witness a trial of the new ammunition, and approval came in time for it to play a valuable role in the latter part of the Peninsular War and at Waterloo in 1815.

Thus it was that at Queenston Heights Winfield Scott, an officer of the United States army and the future conquerer of Mexico, joined the ranks of those who had discovered the effectiveness of Lieutenant Shrapnel's shell. By the end of the day, he and a thousand of his men were prisoners of war; the safety of Upper Canada was no longer in serious doubt.

Throughout the next two years, artillery played its part, with varying degrees of success, from the St. Lawrence to the Upper Great Lakes. The 9-pounders of the Kingston defences took on the 24- and 32-pounders of seven American ships that sought unsuccessfully to destroy the warship HMS *Royal George* in harbour there. The guns, and the gunners, were less successful at York when the destruction of the fort, through the accidental ignition of a powder magazine by a gunner's quickmatch, opened the way for the invaders to capture the town. By the end of 1813 Buffalo had been occupied by British troops, but there was still some sharp fighting ahead.

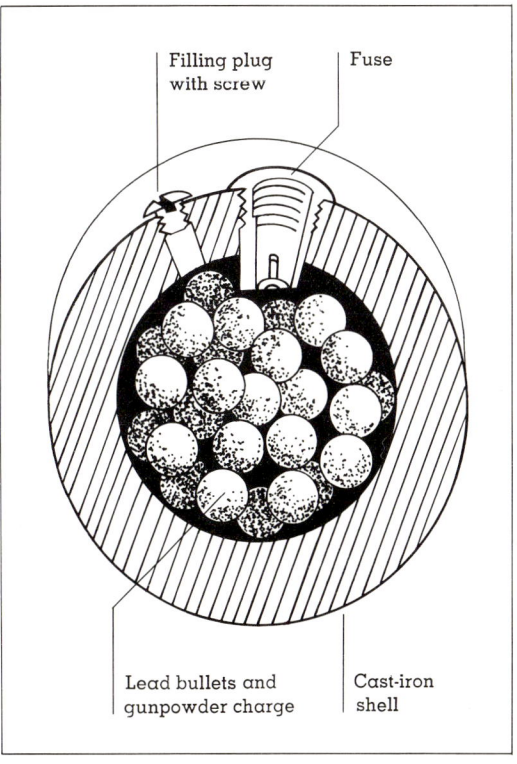

27 An early design of Shrapnel's shell

28 Pattison light 3-pounder brass gun, c. 1775, typical of the smaller brass guns of the period (Coll.: Corporation of the County of Lanark, Perth, Ont.)

In October 1813, Shrapnel's "spherical case-shot", fired by three 6-pounder field guns, had again played a useful part in breaking up an American advance, this time at Crysler's Farm. It was at Lundy's Lane, on 26 October 1814, however, that a still newer invention was introduced on North American battlefields: a Congreve rocket struck and wounded American General Jacob Brown.

Congreve and His Rockets

Rockets of one sort or another had been appearing and disappearing from military arsenals for hundreds of years; in fact, their invention probably preceded that of guns. Asia was usually considered to be their natural home, but, whether in the East or the West, they were normally looked upon as little more than glorified fireworks of only marginal military significance. The change in this outlook began in Mysore, where in 1799 there were many casualties among the soldiers of the East India Company as the result of rockets fired at them by the Indian forces during the siege of Seringapatam.

The news from India received unusually rapid consideration by the Board of Ordnance in London; instructions went out to find out more about the new weapon and to consider the possibility of its being supplied to the British army. The East India Company was not able to provide much information, but the Royal Laboratory at Woolwich, equally ignorant about the device, at least served as the informal channel through which the Board of Ordnance ultimately received better advice. General Sir William Congreve, the Comptroller of the Laboratory, apparently discussed the problem with his son William, who was both a colonel in the Hanoverian army and one of that breed of amateur scientists which flourished in the eighteenth century.

That his father's experts had proved to be uninformed did not deter him. On the contrary, it seems to have provided him with the challenge to both master the theory of rocketry and plan its practical application. Like Shrapnel before him, Congreve had to finance his own early experimental work. Within five years he had increased the range of his test rockets from 500 to 3,000 yards, achieving an accuracy comparable, when they were at their best, to that of the guns of his time. He designed shrapnel and incendiary warheads, in addition to explosive types, for a family of rockets weighing from 6 to 32 pounds. The advantages Congreve claimed for his rockets were demonstrated in action in 1806, when several hundred of them were fired into Boulogne from a flotilla of small craft in the English Channel. The little vessels were able to deliver a volume of firepower that would have been quite beyond their capability had they had to depend on the use of heavy recoiling guns to launch their projectiles.

Within a few years, rockets were being used in land actions as well as in seaborne attacks. The outcome of the Battle of Leipzig in 1813 was significantly influenced by the activities of Britain's one contribution to the allied army—a half troop of the Royal Horse Artillery equipped with Congreve's rockets. To this day, a battery of the Royal Horse Artillery is known as the Rocket Troop in honour of its predecessor's outstanding services at Waterloo.

So it was that, in 1814, rockets contributed to the rout of United States forces at Bladensburg, guarding the way to Washington and thus to the capture of Washington itself. Francis Scott Key witnessed "the rocket's red glare, the bombs bursting in air" over Baltimore, which the British attacked during their return to the coast, and his memory of them is perpetuated in the poem he wrote that later became the American national anthem. The rockets were Congreve rockets, the bombs shrapnel.

Rifling and Breech-Loading: Armstrong and Whitworth

Most of the essentials of modern artillery were known long before they were applied to service weapons and their ammunition. This lag continued even through the Industrial Revolution, at a time when new inventions and methods were being rapidly incorporated into the industrial process. The fact was that the economic and other incentives stimulating manufacture and commerce during the late eighteenth and early nineteenth centuries did not lead to comparable innovations in the military sphere.

In Europe, war was largely an art, waged according to precedents and rituals. The successful general was usually a master of the rules of manoeuvre; he was not a scientific innovator. In the clash of battle, the effective weapons were those which could successfully play a largely predetermined role in a set-piece engagement. The simple smooth-bore, muzzle-loading brass 6-pounders of the British Horse Artillery and the 9-pounders of the Field Artillery met this requirement throughout the long struggle against revolutionary France—from the Low Countries, through the Iberian Peninsula, to Waterloo.

29 A 9-pounder brass gun on a field carriage; manufactured in India but similar to those used at Waterloo (Coll.: Rotunda Museum, Woolwich, England)

Spanning the gap between discovery and practical application was made difficult enough by the military thinking of the time; it was often rendered almost impossible by the limitations of the prevailing mechanical techniques. Machine-making is the essence of engineering, but the carpenters and the blacksmiths, who were the eighteenth-century predecessors of the specialist machine-makers, lacked both the skills and the facilities needed to build efficient machinery. James Watt had to accept cylinders for his steam engines that were often an eighth of an inch wider at one end than at the other. The gun, too, is an engine that uses heat to convert chemical energy into motion; but owing to the conditions of pressure and temperature it operates under, improvements in its performance made even greater demands on engineering ability.

The advantage of the simple cannonball was that it was stable in flight when fired from a smooth-bored gun, but a pointed, elongated projectile would offer less resistance to the air. It had been known for centuries that elongated projectiles could be stabilized in flight, and hence given greater accuracy and range, by the expedient of spinning them (the flights on the projectiles fired by Genoese crossbowmen in the fourteenth century were arranged to produce this very effect). Proposals for rifling the barrels of guns to impart spin had been put forward on many occasions, but the military authorities showed little enthusiasm for the change, and in any case the gun-makers could not produce them. Some small rifled pieces of foreign design were tested by the Ordnance Select Committee in 1850. The results were encouraging, but the army resisted change and the matter was not pursued.

Four years later, Britain was at war with Russia in the Crimea. That shockingly ill-managed affair taught the generals many lessons. One of them was that field guns capable of shaking even Napoleon's veteran troops at Waterloo were of little use against an enemy whose infantry was armed with rifled muskets that outranged them. The solution came almost immediately from a lawyer-turned-engineer named William Armstrong. He had heard that the outcome of the Battle of Inkerman (Crimean War) had remained in doubt until the gunners manning two British smooth-bore 18-pounders had, by dint of great bravery and physical strength, dragged their 2¾-ton pieces through the mud until they were in range of a powerful Russian battery, which they eventually silenced. The obvious need, as Armstrong saw it, was for guns that were lighter, had greater range, and were more accurate than anything the army then possessed. In 1856, Armstrong produced a 5-pounder rifled gun that met all these criteria. Three years later a 12-pounder version was issued to the Field Artillery and a 6-pounder to the Royal Horse Artillery. By the end of the decade, the British army had what were probably the best field artillery weapons in the world.

30 A 6-pounder Armstrong gun, c. 1860
(Coll.: Canadian War Museum)

Armstrong's guns were revolutionary in many respects. Their barrels were made of wrought, rather than cast, iron, and were strengthened by having ingeniously designed jackets shrunk onto them. The twisted rifling consisted of numerous grooves, and the elongated projectiles were coated with lead to permit the rifling to cut into them and impart rotation. Another break with tradition, and one that in practice proved the most difficult to accomplish, was Armstrong's rejection of muzzle-loading for a novel form of breech-loading. The basic idea of breech-loading, as we have seen, was almost as old as guns themselves, but the practical engineering problems had never been satisfactorily overcome. Even Armstrong's plug-and-screw solution, with its copper sealing cup, was perhaps the least satisfactory part of his design.

Armstrong was not alone in his endeavours to apply the full potential of mid-nineteenth-century technical knowledge to gun design. Joseph Whitworth, whose name lives on in the system of standard screw threads he invented, designed a breech-loading gun that spun its projectiles by means of a twisted bore of polygonal form. The performance of this weapon was superior to even that of the Armstrong models.

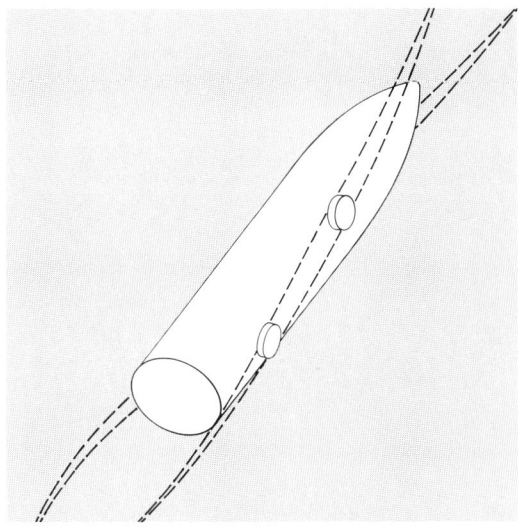

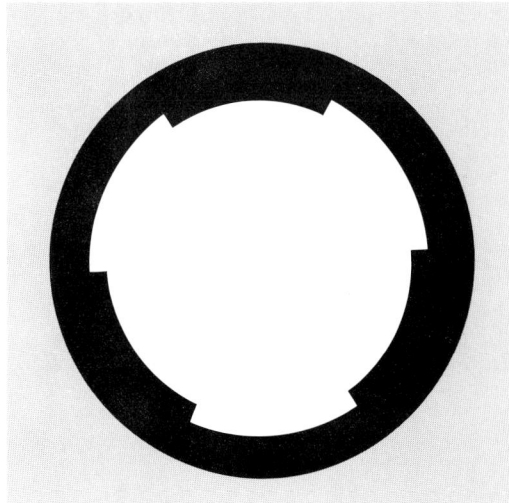

The Demise of the Smooth-Bore: Palliser

Not long after the new guns came into use, a peculiar combination of conservative nostalgia for the simplicity of the old smooth-bore muzzle-loaders, together with the practical problems being experienced with the breech-closing mechanisms of the new weapons, led to at least a partial retreat to the older concepts and to the advent of rifled muzzle-loaders. The pointed shells used with these weapons were fitted either with studs, which slid down the three grooves of the rifling (both on loading and on firing), or with large copper sealing cups, which expanded under the pressure of the burning powder. The inventor of the studded shell, an artillery officer named William Palliser, also developed a practical method of converting smooth-bore guns into rifled pieces by the insertion of wrought-iron liners. By the mid 1870s, the breech-loading gun had faded out of the picture as far as the British army was concerned. A new rifled muzzle-loading (R.M.L.) 9-pounder was designed at Woolwich for both the horse and field batteries. It was acclaimed as equal in performance and superior in reliability when compared with the breech-loading field pieces favoured by the artillery of some of the European powers. In 1873, the first of the new R.M.L. 9-pounders began to arrive in Canada. Before the decade was over, they had been issued to the sixteen militia field batteries and to the batteries of the recently formed Permanent Force.

31/32 A studded shot of Palliser design, and cross-section of a rifled bore with three grooves

33 R.M.L. 9-pounder field gun, c. 1880 (Coll.: Fort Battleford National Historic Park, Sask.)

The Canadian R.M.L. 9-pounders saw action with General Sir Frederick Middleton during the Northwest Rebellion in 1885: they fired case and shrapnel at Fish Creek and gave supporting fire at Batoche. Prior to Cut Knife Hill, one battery had temporarily replaced its 9-pounders with fascinating relics of an earlier age in the form of rifled muzzle-loading 7-pounders made of bronze. These pieces had originated as smooth-bore 3-pounders of a design primarily intended for manufacture in India as mule-borne mountain guns. After they had been bored out and rifled, six of them were sent to Canada in 1870 for the Red River Campaign. Fifteen years later their venerable carriages collapsed from age and wood-rot on the battlefield of Cut Knife Hill.

The conversion of smooth-bore guns to rifled pieces was not limited to the mobile weapons of the field army. Coastal defence and fortress equipment was similarly treated. Palliser's techniques were applied to guns at Victoria, Kingston, Quebec, Lévis, Halifax and Saint John, and smooth-bore 32-pounders became rifled muzzle-loading 64-pounders. Good shooting was subsequently reported at the then respectable range of 2,000 yards.

However, the eclipse of the breech-loader was not permanent. Its obvious advantages—the Ordnance Select Committee was able to list eleven in 1868—were such that its return was almost inevitable once the engineering problems associated with sealing the breech had been solved. The breakthrough was made by the French with the development of the de Bange obturator (closure) system, which has remained essentially unchanged to this day. The return to breech-loading designs was further hastened by the disastrous explosion of a 12-inch R.M.L. Palliser gun on board HMS *Thunderer* in 1879. Subsequent investigations at the Proof and Experimental Establishment at Woolwich showed that the gun had been accidentally double-shotted, which could not have occurred with a breech-loading weapon. Eventually the designation *breech-loading* became associated with weapons sealed in accordance with the de Bange or similar obturator systems. When the charge is loaded in a brass (or steel) cartridge case, which subsequently serves to seal the breech mechanism from the rearward flow of gas, the gun is usually referred to as being a *quick-firing* type.

34 Laying a R.M.L. Palliser fortress gun for line at Quebec, c. 1890

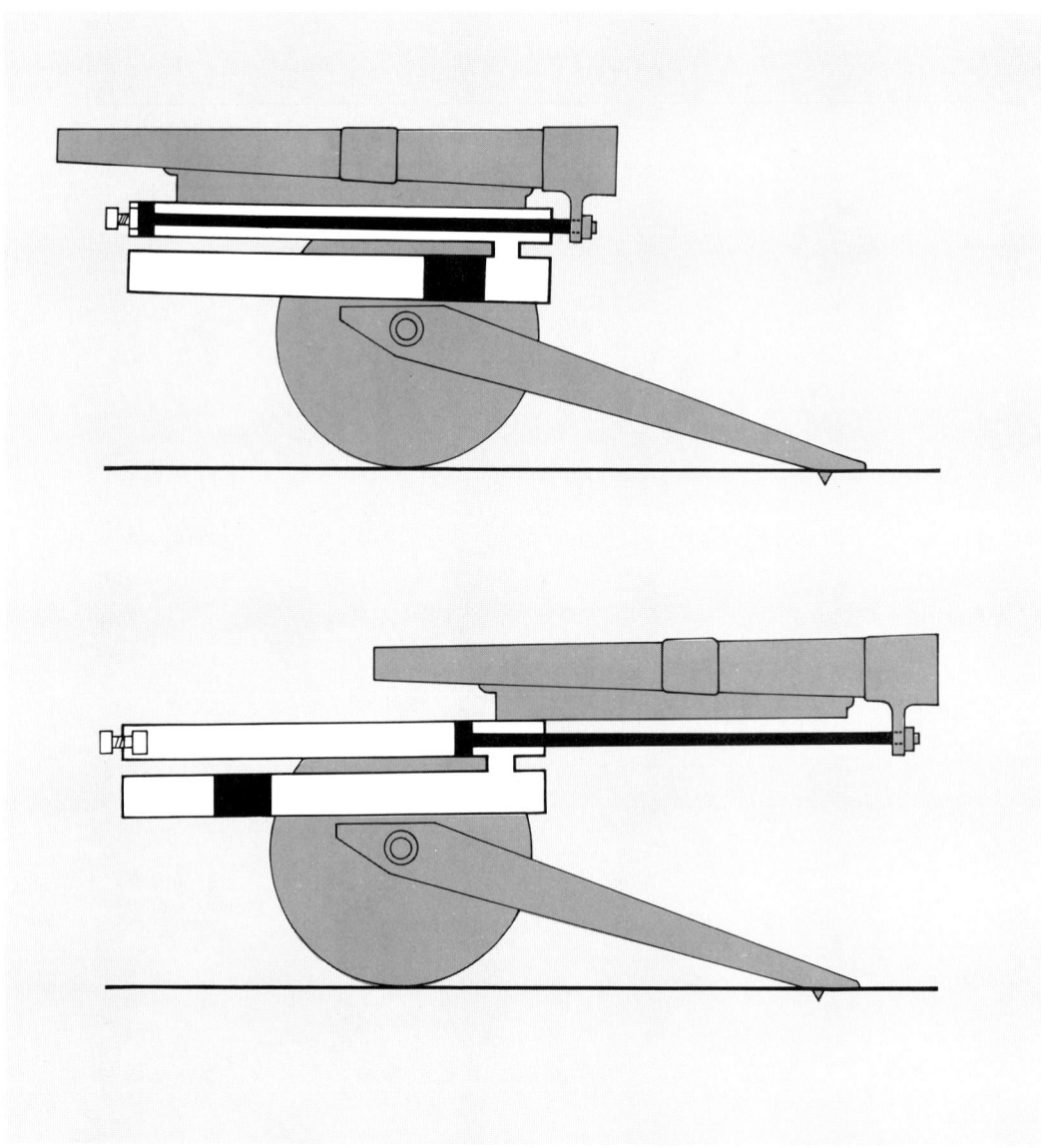

35 The principle of the simple recoil system

Steel Barrels and Anti-Recoil Devices

In 1740, Britain was producing some 18,000 tons of iron a year; a century later the output had risen almost a hundredfold. Nevertheless, brass remained a popular metal for the manufacture of gun barrels until well into the nineteenth century. In September 1815, it was the glitter of the sun on the brass field-pieces of the allied armies deployed around the Place du Carrousel that persuaded the citizens of Paris that Wellington would bode no interference with his plans to restore to their rightful owners the art treasures Napoleon had plundered. Although both cast and wrought iron had been used by gun-makers for hundreds of years, the theoretical advantages of iron did not always offset the manufacturing problems it posed. So it was with steel. By the middle of the nineteenth century, steel began to flow from Henry Bessemer's new converters and from William Siemens's open-hearth furnaces. It was no longer a semiprecious substance, but was available both cheaply and in ever-increasing quantities. Again, the problem was one of manufacturing techniques; it was well towards the close of the century before the gun-makers were able to reap the potential advantages of steel.

Long before schoolchildren were taught that to every action there is an equal and opposite reaction, gunners had learned to live with the practical implications of recoil. The alternatives available to them were limited. They could either attach their piece to a mounting so massive, so firmly anchored or so steeply angled that its recoil was inconsiderable, or they could let a wheeled carriage run backwards after each round and then drag it forward into position for the next shot. It was well into the second half of the nineteenth century before methods began to be developed to absorb and control the violence of recoil. Originally, these various hydraulic and pneumatic devices were so massive that their use was generally limited to fortress installations. The French changed that situation in 1897 with their famous 75-millimetre gun. Not only was this gun light enough for field use, but it was designed to allow the barrel to return to the fully run-out position after absorbing the energy of the initial recoil.

36 French quick-firing 75-mm field gun (Coll.: Canadian War Museum)

Propellants, Projectiles and High Explosives

As guns changed almost beyond recognition during the last half of the nineteenth century, so did the ammunition they fired. Again, the advances came in part from the new ability to apply existing knowledge, in part from the determination of soldier-inventors to overcome deficiencies in the equipment they were issued.

The simple, tubular, powder-filled time-fuse, ignited originally by a portfire and later by the powder gases that always escaped past a round projectile in a smooth-bore gun, had remained unchanged in principle since it was used at the siege of Bonifacio, Corsica, in 1421. It was not until 1855 that the first important improvement occurred—the introduction of Colonel E. M. Boxer's design. Boxer was a prolific inventor whose contributions ranged from improved shrapnel shell to parachute flares. His fuse consisted of powder rings that could be ignited through holes pierced, before firing, at premarked positions, each of which was equivalent to half a second.

Controlled burning times of up to 20 seconds were eventually available. This design was effective as long as there was sufficient windage between the shell and the bore for the propellant gases to leak forward and ignite the fuse. When rifled guns with improved bore-sealing came along, another method had to be found. Fortunately, an amateur chemist had produced the key to solving this problem three-quarters of a century earlier.

In March 1800, Edward Howard startled his colleagues at a meeting of the Royal Society in London by demonstrating the properties of his "new fulminating mercury". This was the latest member of an unstable family of salts whose propensity to detonate when struck led to their being given a name derived from the Latin word *fulmen*, meaning "lightning". A century and a half earlier, the diarist Samuel Pepys had recorded his fascination with an experiment in which the detonation of a pinch of silver fulminate destroyed the bowl of a spoon. Howard's contribution was to discover a member of this peculiar family that could be produced in forms insensitive enough to have practical application. Later in the century, mercury fulminate was joined by another and more convenient chemical, of somewhat similar properties, known as lead azide. With these convenient materials available, it was not too difficult to develop methods of igniting the powder train of Boxer's time-fuse through the shock produced by the propellant charge. Similarly, percussion fuses could be designed that would cause shells to burst through a chain of reactions set off by the activation of a small detonator on impact.

The discovery of chemicals that, upon being struck, are capable of initiating the burning of propellants and the detonation of other explosives not only facilitated the design of modern fuses, it also permitted the development of new methods of firing guns. At Waterloo the field guns were still being fired by the application of a quick-match to a touch-hole filled with gunpowder. It is true that the powder was contained in goose quills and was no longer poured loose, but an external source of flame had to be applied, as it had for five hundred years. The coming of lead azide and mercury fulminate permitted the gunpowder in the chamber to be ignited by means of a blow rather than a match. In the breech-loading system, as it was eventually developed, the charge received its flash from a tube containing powder that had itself been ignited by the striking of a percussion cap. The quick-firing system uses a similar principle; a primer that contains a powder magazine and an activating cap is screwed into the base of the cartridge case.

There were two other chemical discoveries that further revolutionized the design of gun ammunition during the closing years of the last century. Together, they relegated the previously all-conquering gunpowder to a minor role on the stage of war. In 1885, experiments were begun in England to evaluate a large number of potential substitutes for gunpowder as a filling for the common shell. The choice fell on picric acid, which had been known for more than a century as the basis for a yellow dye. For security reasons it was referred to as *lyddite,* trials having been carried out on the artillery ranges at Lydd. The French, calling it *melinite,* were already using the new explosive, as were the Germans and the Japanese, though they too had their own confidential names for it. Lyddite was much more powerful than gunpowder, but it had many unpleasant characteristics. By the outbreak of the First World War, the decision had been taken in England to change from lyddite to a somewhat less powerful but more amenable filling known as T.N.T., or trinitrotoluene, which, incidentally, the Germans had already been using for more than a decade.

37 The axle spade of the B.L. 12-pounder 6-cwt. gun (Coll.: Canadian War Museum)

While gunpowder was being replaced as a shell-filling by the new high explosives, it was also losing its monopoly as a propellant to various compositions based on nitrocellulose. The first in the field was a mixture of various types of nitrocellulose, known as *Poudre B,* developed by the Frenchman Paul Vieille in 1884. Within a few years, Frederick Abel and James Dewar in Britain had invented a method of blending nitrocellulose with nitroglycerine and pressing the resultant dough through small circular dies. The cords thus produced gave rise to what has tended to become almost a generic name for modern gun propellants—cordite. In addition to having significant ballistic advantages over gunpowder, cordite offered the great tactical advantage of being relatively smokeless. It did, however, have one great disadvantage: the gases that it generated during burning were much hotter than those released by gunpowder and gave rise to massive erosion of the gun barrel. In 1901 a modified cordite was introduced, and it gradually replaced the original formula. It contained more nitrocellulose and less nitroglycerine than its predecessor, and was distinctly less erosive. Among the tests given to the new cordites before their acceptance into the service was exposure to climatic extremes in various parts of the Empire. The sample that had been stored through a Quebec winter performed satisfactorily.

New Calibres and Carriages

The rifled muzzle-loading 9-pounder continued in service with the Canadian Militia field batteries for more than twenty-five years, and it was not until 1897 that the first of the new generation of weapons began to arrive in the form of the breech-loading 12-pounder 6-hundredweight. This weapon had been issued to the Royal Horse Artillery in Britain in 1894, while a similar but somewhat heavier piece, firing a 15-pound shell, had been supplied to the British Field Batteries. The 12-pounder, with the aid of a cordite charge, could fire its forged-steel shrapnel shell 5,600 yards—2,000 yards beyond the range of the R.M.L. 9-pounder. The availability of the new No. 56 fuse enabled this shell to be detonated at a preset time or on impact. The one round was therefore considered to be a convenient substitute for both the earlier shrapnel and the old powder-filled common shell. The steel carriages were lighter and more robust than those the Canadian gunners had previously become accustomed to, but they still had a serious recoil problem. The original design had recoil-control

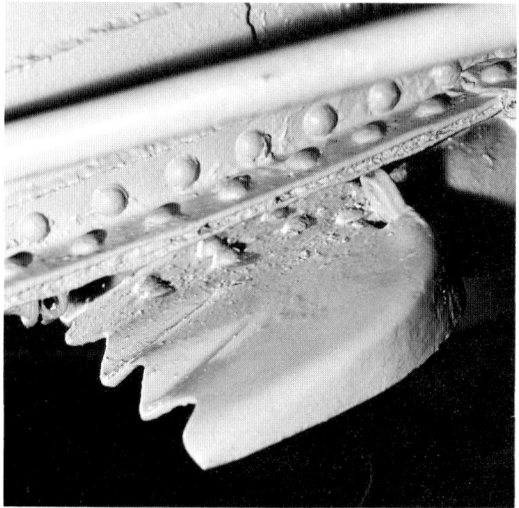

wedges that were fitted under the wheels during firing; nevertheless, the gun still had to be relaid between rounds (the procedure whereby a gun-layer calculates elevation, etc., to aim the shell at the target—sometimes unseen). A subsequent modification provided for the attachment of a mechanical device called a spade, fitted to the gun so that it would dig into the ground on firing to curb recoil; but this was still a far from satisfactory solution.

When the South African War broke out in 1899, Sir Wilfrid Laurier, Prime Minister of Canada, decided, after much Parliamentary debate, that some tangible support for the Empire's effort was required. Canada's contribution included three artillery batteries, each equipped with six of the new breech-loading 12-pounder guns. It was two of these Canadian pieces that played such a dramatic part in the action at Leliefontein on 7 November 1900. In conjunction with the Royal Canadian Dragoons, the gunners fought a gallant rearguard action against a determined attack by Boer cavalry aimed at capturing the guns. At times the 12-pounders were seriously endangered, but before the day was out the enemy attack wilted under fire at point-blank range and the gun detachments managed to disengage. The guns were saved, and three Canadians had won Victoria Crosses.

38 One of the B.L. 12-pounder 6-cwt. guns that were in action at Leliefontein (Coll.: Canadian War Museum)

**Canada Abroad:
Science Goes to War**

4

39 (p. 64) Alfred Bastien, *Canadian Gunners in the Mud, Passchendaele* (detail), oil on canvas, 1918 (Coll.: Canadian War Museum)

The field gun is an 18-pounder.

40 Q.F. 18-pounder field gun (Coll.: Canadian War Museum)

The Gun of the Western Front

The Canadian National War Memorial in Ottawa is at all times an evocative piece of sculpture. Seen through the softening veil of an early autumn mist, it can assume a mystic feeling of movement that belies its solid mass. In a moment of changing light, the field gun seems almost to lurch forward down the rutted track in response to the united efforts of its team. That this type of gun should have been given so prominent a place in the national monument seems both natural and historically justifiable. With the exception of the Lee Enfield rifle, there is no other weapon more symbolic of Canadian arms during the First World War than the 18-pounder field gun. For more than four years, from the morning of 2 March 1915, when the first Canadian shell was fired in France, until 28 May 1919, when the 67th Battery Canadian Field Artillery ceased fire in northern Russia, the 18-pounders—sometimes singly, sometimes in dozens, and sometimes by the hundreds—had supported the infantry, faithfully and reliably, in advance and in retreat. During the course of the war, the Commonwealth armies fired nearly 100 million 18-pounder rounds. Yet the original decision to accept the gun into the armouries of the Crown had hinged on the casting of a single tie-breaking vote.

The Lessons of the Boer War

The South African War taught the British army many lessons, some of which were learned at tragic cost. The tactics, the equipment and even the uniforms of the regiments that sailed to fight in yet one more colonial war had varied ancestries. They were based in part on the practices of the Napoleonic Wars, in part on the need to garrison the Indian subcontinent, and in part on the varied experiences of a dozen-and-one minor wars, including the Crimean, fought in distant and often barely accessible parts of the world. These influences often produced solutions that were remarkably unsuited to the conditions British and Canadian troops faced when they landed in South Africa. Fighting the skilful, fast-moving and forever disappearing Boer commandos across the wide expanses of the High Veldt called for very different methods than those which had been successful against the massed ranks of the Old Guard at Waterloo, the spears of the Zulu *impis,* or the muskets of the tribesmen of the Khyber Pass. Discipline and tradition were often the only reply the British troops could make to this novel enemy.

In the end, the lessons were learned and victory was achieved, but thousands of needless graves lay under the African sun. One of the most important of those lessons was that the weapons most British and Canadian artillery batteries were equipped with were obsolescent, as were the tactics governing their use.

The standard practice was for the field guns to come into action in the open, usually in full view of the enemy, much as their predecessors had acted during Wellington's campaigns against Napoleon. The response of the Boers was often in the form of either accurate fire from their Mauser rifles, directed against the gun detachments and their horses, or artillery fire from weapons that, while far fewer in number, outranged and generally outperformed the British field pieces. The scattered Boers normally presented difficult targets, even when within range, and when they did cluster together they were as likely as not to be behind the stone parapets of well-located encampments, which provided good protection against the shrapnel that constituted virtually the only ammunition available to the British field batteries.

In November 1899, a young war correspondent arrived in South Africa to report on the campaign for the London *Morning Post*. Within a matter of months he was sharing his concern about artillery with his readers. He wanted to know why the armies of the Empire did not have field guns with fixed ammunition and 8,000-yards range, capable of matching the weapons of the Boers'

Staatsartillerie. He was equally concerned that senior British officers appeared to regard the superior performance of the enemy's guns with little more than scientific curiosity, and that thousands of British shells seemed to have virtually no effect on the Boer riflemen as they poured their devastating fire down the slopes of Spion Kop. Well might he advise the English artillery experts to "please note and if possible copy" as he reported on the performance of an enemy battery, 7,000 yards away, which dropped a shell close to a small group of horsemen galloping across the veldt. Forty years later, equally pointed requests for action to improve the effectiveness of the weapons of the British army were to flow once again from the now more influential pen of Prime Minister Winston Churchill.

41 H.P. Wilson, *Colenso, 15 December 1899—Saving the Guns*, watercolour (Coll.: Parker Gallery, London)
British artillery in action in South Africa.

42 Q.F. 13-pounder field gun (Coll.: Canadian War Museum)

A New Gun At Last

Fortunately, there were a number of senior officers at the front and in London who were as concerned as Churchill at the obsolescence of both the guns and the tactics of the artillery. Before the war was over, General Sir Henry Brackenbury, who later was to become Director General of Ordnance, had been instructed to examine the whole sorry story and to make appropriate recommendations. In an age when innovativeness was not considered a very desirable attribute in a British general, Brackenbury was a fortunate choice for this vital task: in many ways his military thinking was a generation ahead of his time.

Drawing on his experience as the military correspondent of *The Times* during the Russo-Turkish Wars, he had advocated the use of armoured mobile artillery in the assault role forty years before the first tanks crawled over the battlefields of the Somme. Within a matter of months, he ordered the weapons of the Horse and Field artilleries to be withdrawn over a three-year period. Knowing that suitable replacements could not be produced by British gun-makers within that period, he took the further unprecedented step of purchasing from a German manufacturer sufficient guns and ammunition to outfit eighteen field batteries. The gun he chose to fill the gap until his own specifications could be met was the famous Ehrhardt 15-pounder. This weapon, capable of firing shrapnel shell to a range of 6,500 yards, had a very effective recoil system and a rate of fire comparable to that of the even more famous French 75-millimetre (the *soixante-quinze*), whose capabilities had become legendary since it first appeared in the closing years of the nineteenth century.

In the event, no single British manufacturer offered a weapon that met all of Brackenbury's requirements. Each, however, offered various desirable features. The pragmatic solution reached was to order some trial guns incorporating the best characteristics of the various competing submissions for both the Horse and Field branches. The barrels were essentially Armstrong-designed, the recoil system had its origin with Vickers, and much of the carriage came from designers in the Royal Arsenal at Woolwich. The result was the quick-firing 13-pounder and its heavier relative the Q.F. 18-pounder.

The main characteristics of the two guns were similar. Both had a maximum range, with shrapnel shell, of 6,200 yards and a rate of fire of up to twenty rounds a minute. Their ammunition was fixed—shell, propellant, cartridge case and means of ignition being loaded as a single unit. They had bulletproof shields as well as sighting systems that permitted indirect fire (in other words, they could engage targets not visible from the gun position). The barrels were of wire-wound construction, in which a single tube was strengthened by steel wire wrapped around it to produce a lighter and a cheaper gun than was possible by using the method then current of building up a barrel by shrinking concentric tubes one upon the other. On firing, the recoiling barrel slid rearwards on guides; its energy was absorbed by a hydraulic buffer and springs, which then returned it to the firing position. The significant difference between the 13- and 18-pounders, apart from overall weight, was in the weight of their shot. The field gun fired an 18.5-pound shell, and the Horse Artillery gun a 13.5- pound projectile. Almost immediately the question arose as to whether the difference was worth the extra problems that would arise from having to maintain two guns in service at the same time: why not standardize on the 13-pounder, which was possibly a little more accurate than the heavier gun, and thus avoid unnecessary duplication? The argument raged, and support seemed to be equally divided between the proponents of the "single-gun" and the "two-gun" policies. In the end, a decision had to be made if production was ever to get started. As the committee of experts was unable to make a firm recommendation one way or the other, Prime Minister Arthur Balfour exercised his vote. It was in favour of the two-gun programme, and the 18-pounder was saved. On Christmas Eve 1904, production orders were placed. The decision was made for the Empire, and the new guns began to arrive in Canada in 1906.

43 An 18-pounder in action in France, 1918

The wisdom of Balfour's choice was to be shown a decade later when, during the four years of the First World War, the heavier guns were to fire some seventy rounds in action for every one fired by the 13-pounders. On 11 November 1918, the Order of Battle of the Canadian Artillery included thirty-five batteries of Field Artillery equipped with 18-pounder guns; there were only three batteries of "Horse guns", including one in the anti-aircraft role.

During the course of the war, this truly ubiquitous field gun and its ammunition underwent numerous changes. It had been designed to provide supporting fire for marching infantry in a brief, mobile war, just as the 13-pounder had been designed to gallop with the cavalry in actions of wide-ranging movement. After the far-too-mobile weeks of the retreat from Mons, this type of warfare was to become almost unknown on the Western Front for the next four years. Instead, the vast majority of the 18-pounders, together with most of the other guns of the Allied armies, were to be committed to a largely static role in which they would pound the aching soil of France and Flanders to help the infantry gain a few hundred yards of rusted wire and battered trenches. The weapons that Brackenbury had ingeniously devised needed many modifications to enable them to meet the demands of this unexpected task.

War in the Mud
The effective range of the original 18-pounders fell far short not only of the 8,000 yards Churchill called for in South Africa, but also of the usual requirements on the battlefields of France. The field batteries could not bring down supporting fire far enough behind the enemy lines and, when an advance did occur, they could not protect the infantry without time-consuming moves forward to new battery positions. There are few weapons systems that come to the end of their service lives without having had their performance improved well beyond their designers' original objectives. So it was with the 18-pounder. By 1918, the maximum range had been increased to over 9,000 yards, 50 per cent greater than the original specifications. Most of this improvement was obtained by changes in carriage design that permitted the gun to be elevated well beyond the original limit of 16 degrees. Further gains came from improvements in the ammunition.

When the Canadian gunners took their 18-pounders into action in 1915, they fired nothing but shrapnel. During the South African War, there had been some suggestion that field guns should be supplied with high-explosive shells as well as with the traditional shrapnel. There was no doubt that the latter was very effective against troops in the open, but there were some who questioned its value against an enemy in a well-protected position. The advocates of shrapnel received unwanted support from the experience with the Boers, who on more than one occasion fired shrapnel shell

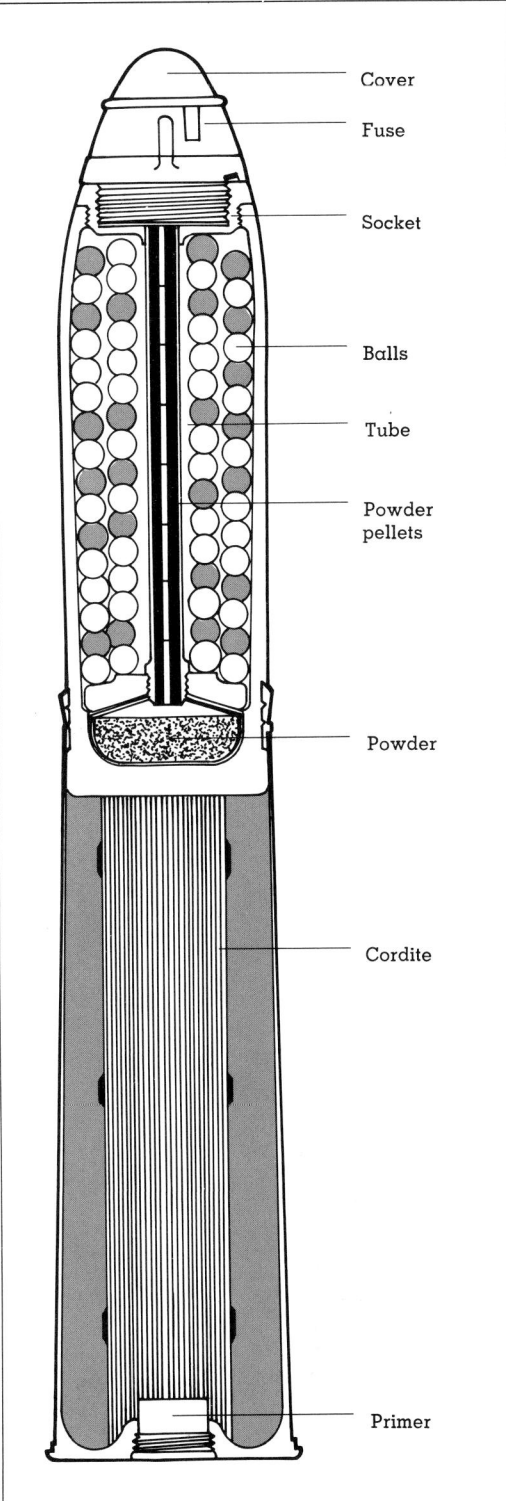

44 A round of 18-pounder shrapnel ammunition

from captured British guns, to the considerable discomfort of the previous owners. So strongly did the General Staff believe that any future European war would be one of rapid movement that in 1914 the case for shrapnel seemed unanswerable. As a result, field guns were equipped with only shrapnel; even the field howitzers carried only 30 per cent of their ammunition in the form of high-explosive shells. The decision seemed to be reasonably well justified during the early months of the war, when 13-pounder and 18-pounder shrapnel was used with considerable effect during the sweeping advance and subsequent withdrawal of the Germany army. The picture began to change when autumn gave way to winter and the armies became bogged down in position-warfare of trenches and barbed wire. Wire was something the advocates of shrapnel had never seriously considered. It was largely impervious to a hail of lead balls, and yet there was nothing else to use against it. Nineteen-fiifteen was the dark year for the guns, of which there were far too few. Disastrous premature bursts, through poor ammunition production, were common. There were serious shortages of ammunition, and what little ammunition there was was ineffective for the tasks to be performed. For example, when Canadian field guns went into action in their first major engagement at Neuve Chapelle in March 1915, they were officially limited to a daily ration of a dozen or so rounds of shrapnel per gun, and had to cease fire for lack of ammunition when the advancing infantry most seriously needed their support. After the battle, the ration for field guns and howitzers was reduced to three rounds a day. In September of that year, half the men of Kitchener's "new army"—the legendary first 100,000 volunteers—were killed or wounded by German machine-gun fire on the uncut barbed wire at Loos.

45 A No. 80 Mark IVA fuse found by William Barnes, the author's father, in a captured German position that had received a direct hit, at Ploegsteert, Belgium, in 1916

46 The principle of a typical time and percussion fuse

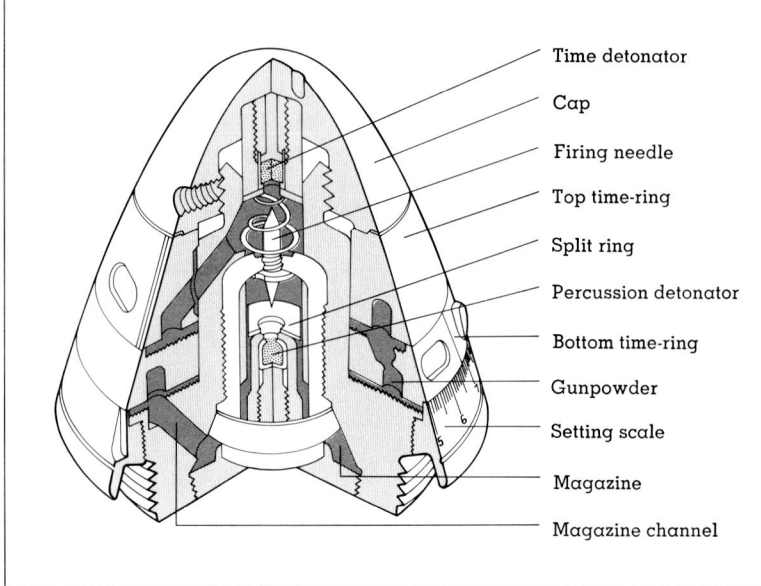

Time detonator
Cap
Firing needle
Top time-ring
Split ring
Percussion detonator
Bottom time-ring
Gunpowder
Setting scale
Magazine
Magazine channel

The first expedient, in response to the gunner's call for a high-explosive shell that would cut wire, was hardly more effective than shrapnel. There simply was no reliable percussion fuse available to detonate the high-explosive shells of the field guns. Time and Percussion Fuse No. 80 was designed to work with shrapnel, but it would not detonate a high-explosive shell. The only fuse capable of doing this, Percussion Fuse No. 44, was a very poor performer. To meet the emergency, a makeshift solution was developed: both fuses were used. The more reliable No. 80 had a No. 44 fitted below it, and when the shell struck its target the first fuse activated the second, which in turn detonated the shell. At least, that was the theory. In practice, the system was likely to result in a failure to explode if the angle of arrival was shallow; if the angle was steeper, the delay in the cumbersome system was such that the shell generally penetrated deeply into the smothering Flanders mud before exploding. There was a desperate need for a fuse that would function reliably at all practical angles of arrival and would detonate a high-explosive shell while it was still aboveground. Fortunately for Canada, the

Design Department at Woolwich developed a brilliantly simple answer to this difficult problem. The resultant Direct Action Percussion Fuse No. 106 became available to the supporting artillery in time to cut the German wire before the Canadian attack on Vimy Ridge. The central feature of this fuse was a strong needle fitted with a mushroom head. Upon impact the needle struck a detonator, which ignited the magazine of the fuse, and this in turn detonated the shell. The design incorporated several simple but effective safety devices to prevent the striker from coming into contact with the detonator before the shell had ceased to accelerate—some way beyond the muzzle of the gun. The fuse was so close to being instantaneous in its operation that the shell exploded almost as soon as it touched the wire or the ground; thus, the crater resulting from the fuse's detonation of a field-gun shell on the ground was often little bigger than a large saucer.

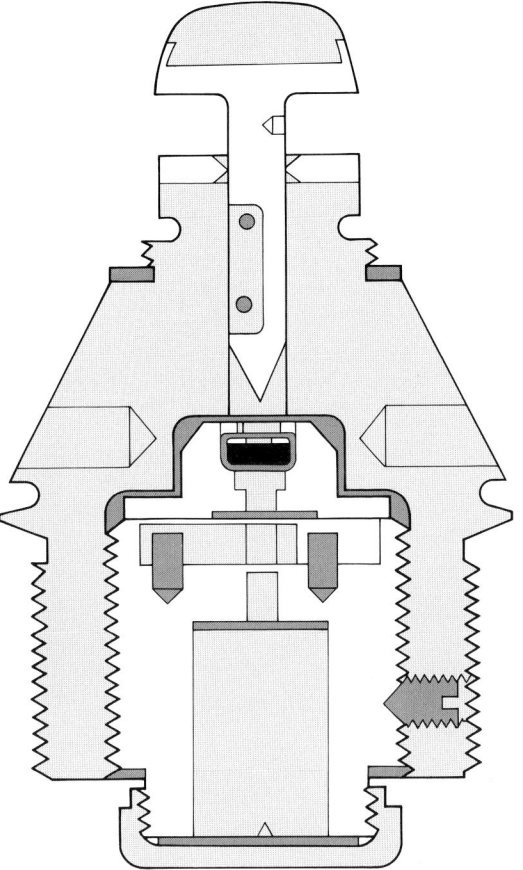

47 Diagram of a No. 106 fuse during flight

48 Q.F. 4.5-inch howitzer

Many of the ammunition problems that plagued the 18-pounders and 13-pounders during the early years of World War I also struck that other mainstay of the Canadian Field Artillery, the quick-firing 4.5-inch howitzer. This weapon, too, was the outcome of the lessons learned during the South African War. Unlike the field guns, however, its design did not result from the marriage of features from competing proposals. The submission put forward by the Coventry Ordnance Works met all the criteria the committee had laid down, and it was accepted as the new field howitzer for the divisional artillery. By the end of the war, each Canadian field artillery brigade included a 4.5-inch howitzer battery together with three 18-pounder batteries. The sturdy howitzer fired a 35-pound shell, which had to be loaded and rammed ahead of the cartridge case containing the propellant charge and the primer. This system (usually referred to as "separate loading" as opposed to the "fixed" ammunition of the field guns) was based on the howitzer's requirement for charges that could be varied in the field—a clearly impossible operation if the shell was firmly fixed in the neck of the cartridge case. By the appropriate combination of elevation and charge, the 4.5-inch howitzer was capable of delivering plunging fire on targets behind crests and in other locations that offered protection from the field guns, with their higher muzzle velocities and flatter trajectories. Although this weapon, with its heavier shell, was designed to deal with earthworks and similar fortifications that were beyond the capacity of the lighter shell of the 13- and 18-pounders, such was the strength of the open-warfare school of thought that 70 per cent of the ammunition it was originally supplied with was shrapnel.

Shell Rationing and the Deadly Prematures

There were many causes for the appalling shell shortages of 1915 and the incidence of deadly prematures (so high, at one stage, that one 18-pounder shell out of every five thousand could be expected to destroy the gun it was fired from). With the exception of a few realists, such as Lord Kitchener, the Minister for War, British military planners were convinced that the duration of the war would be measured in terms of months. In August 1914, few doubted that the fighting would be over by Christmas, and ammunition supplies were planned accordingly. Not only did the months turn into years, but the amount of ammunition expended under conditions of static warfare was vastly greater than the planners had envisaged. While the requirements for ammunition soared to unimagined levels, production suffered from equally unexpected setbacks. Labour strife in Britain, often fomented by radical minorities, led to strikes in munitions plants. The ready acceptance of skilled craftsmen into the army without regard to the effect on defence production had the inevitable adverse results on both quality and output. On top of all this, the failure to recognize the possibility of a long war led to guns and ammunition being designed with little regard to the economic and technical problems that prolonged hostilities might bring. No serious attempt was made to develop simple mass-production methods that would place minimum demands on scarce resources of skilled manpower and raw materials. Nowhere was this failure more obvious than in the production of artillery fuses. While the slaughter of Loos was in progress, there were 25 million 18-pounder shells lying useless in factories and depots for lack of No. 80 fuses.

49 Spent cartridge cases after the attack on Vimy Ridge, May 1917

The Beginnings of Canada's Arms Industry

Canada had only one gun-ammunition plant in production when the nation went to war in August 1914. The old Dominion Arsenal in Quebec City, which had been manufacturing shells of various types since the turn of the century, started to produce 18-pounder shrapnel shells and cartridge cases in 1910. Unfortunately, the quality of manufacture left much to be desired—oval projectiles, loose driving bands, anything-but-circular shrapnel balls, and shell bodies with unacceptable metallurgical defects. All in all, the ammunition was described as being potentially more dangerous to the friendly troops it might be fired over than to the enemy! This state of affairs came to light in 1913, and vigorous steps were taken to rectify the situation. An inspectorate was established, independent of the Arsenal authorities, to check and test, and when war came a year later, Canada could offer Britain 4,000 shells a week. At first the fuses were made in the United States, but the Minister of Militia's Shell Committee soon set about finding Canadian firms willing to undertake their manufacture. By the end of February 1915, they had shipped 81,222 shells overseas. By then, excellent control ensured good quality, and regular proof-firings were carried out at Petite-Rivière and at Valcartier military camp near Quebec City. Thirty years later, the odd shrapnel ball from these early trials could still be found on the slopes of Pinkney Mountain (now called mont Triquet), which loomed over the extensive facilities of a modern Artillery Proof and Development Establishment that had been built up on the site of the primitive test range of the First World War.

As the demand for artillery ammunition grew beyond all expectations, the Shell Committee, and later the Imperial Munitions Board, combed Canada's industries to find plants capable of mastering the techniques and meeting the extremely high standards associated with ammunition production. Very few of the firms approached to make 15-pounder and 18-pounder shrapnel shells, for instance, realized at first that eighty different gauges would be needed for each design, in addition to the regular chemical and metallurgical examination of raw materials. The Russell Motor Car Company of Toronto manufactured the No. 80 fuse in large quantities, but the dimensions were so critical that for every 100 operators on the production line the company had to employ 50 inspectors, in addition to the 10 examiners provided by the government. The apparently simple brass cartridge cases for field guns and howitzers necessitated more than thirty separate operations, ranging from punching to annealing and from drawing to tapering. Achieving the right metal hardness at various critical parts of the case walls was essential; otherwise the case was liable either to fail on firing (and thus permit the hot gases from the propellant to pour backwards and ruin the gun chamber) or to seal so tightly that the case could not be extracted, with the result that the gun was put out of action.

Naturally there were many problems in the early days, and the product of a good deal of hard work and enthusiasm often finished up on the scrap pile under the rejection stamp of the inspectorate. In an amazingly short time, however, Canadian ammunition began to be shipped overseas in enormous quantities. By the end of 1917, Canada was producing more than half the 18-pounder shrapnel shells then required by the British Ministry of Munitions, and a critical re-examination of a massive sample at Woolwich found that only a third of one per cent were in any way defective. In addition to field-gun ammunition, Canada's factories manufactured shells of many other types, up to and including those for the 9.2-inch howitzers of the heaviest siege batteries of the Canadian Corps.

At war's end, Canada had shipped more than 25 million shells, 41 million complete rounds, 48 million cartridge cases, and 148 million pounds of high explosives and propellants. This impressive contribution to the eventual success of the Allied cause became even more remarkable when viewed against what had seemed an optimistic promise of 4,000 shells a week, made only four years earlier.

A Renaissance in Siege Warfare

The prevailing doctrine of a short, fast-moving war naturally gave little place to heavy artillery, which by its very nature was relatively immobile, and was designed primarily for bombarding fixed fortifications. The European powers, unlike the British, had developed tactical doctrines that envisaged the use of heavy artillery in a more mobile role than it had traditionally played in siege operations. Even in the siege function, the German and Austrian armies had made major improvements in the use of heavy artillery. The first demonstration came in August 1914, when the Germans battered the supposedly impregnable Belgian fortresses to pieces in a matter of days with their 42-centimetre howitzers—the Big Berthas—, aided by the equally formidable Austrian Schlanke Emmas.

50 B.L. 60-pounder in action in France during the First World War

51 B.L. 6-inch 26-cwt. howitzer

The British and Canadian forces did, however, have a very useful gun of medium calibre, which again was the direct outcome of the South African experience. The Boer artillery had shown the value of fairly mobile weapons that could fire a shell of effective size against troop concentrations and other targets beyond the range of normal field pieces. The answer was the Armstrong breech-loading 60-pounder gun, which met the proposed range and firepower specifications and could still be pulled by a team of horses. This accurate and reliable weapon fired both shrapnel and high-explosive shells to ranges in the order of 10,000 yards—a performance subsequently increased by improvements in ammunition design. The 60-pounder provided the basic equipment of the Canadian heavy batteries throughout most of the war.

The medium howitzer of the British army in 1914 was of pre–Boer War vintage, obsolete in virtually every sense. The breech-loading 6-inch 30-hundredweight equipment had to be unshipped from its main travelling carriage and mounted on a ground platform for firing, a slow and laborious process at best, and appallingly difficult under the conditions on the Western Front. Even when it had been brought into action, its range of barely 7,000 yards imposed severe limitations on its usefulness. Its replacement was the breech-loading 6-inch 26-hundredweight howitzer, designed by Vickers in a matter of weeks, which began to arrive in France in the winter of 1915. Not only could this weapon be fired off its wheeled carriage, it was also supplied with a very well-designed set of propellant charges that enabled it to bring accurate fire to bear on virtually any target within its eventual range of 11,000 yards—and this without serious problems of crest clearance, that is, in directing fire on the further side of hills. By 1918, eight Canadian siege batteries were equipped with the 6-inch 26-hundredweight howitzer, which continued its useful service life well into the Second World War.

52 Kenneth Forbes, *Canadian Artillery in Action*, oil on canvas, 1918 (Coll.: Canadian War Museum)

The weapon is a B.L. 6-inch 26-cwt. howitzer at the Somme, July 1916.

53 B.L. 9.2-inch howitzer emplaced

54 B.L. 9.2-inch howitzer in action in France during the First World War

As the battle lines in France became ever more static, the enemy had the opportunity to build underground fortifications of a strength probably without precedent in field engineering. It became clear that siege artillery of comparable fortress-smashing capacity would therefore be needed in the field. A larger version of the successful 6-inch howitzer was produced with a calibre of 8 inches, but this was not enough. Fortunately, the designers at the Coventry Ordnance Works, the originators of the quick-firing 4.5-inch howitzer, had produced a prototype 9.2-inch weapon in June 1914.

The howitzer and its mounting travelled in three sections, each weighing in the order of four and one-half tons and towed by a traction engine. It was anything but mobile, and took at least twelve hours to be brought into action. Nevertheless, it threw a 290-pound shell with considerable effect. The single experimental weapon, which came to be known as "Mother", was shipped off to France and fired its first offensive rounds during the Battle of Neuve Chapelle in support of the British First Army, of which the artillery of the newly arrived First Canadian Division formed a part. The 9.2-inch howitzer, somewhat modified by this experience, was put into full-scale production, and eventually twelve of these pieces were manned by the gunners of two Canadian siege batteries. The memory of this massive weapon is still preserved in Jagger's starkly effective Royal Artillery Memorial at Hyde Park Corner in London.

Towards the end of the war, some of the German fortifications proved to be beyond the capacity of even the 9.2-inch howitzer; the pillboxes that faced the Canadians at Passchendaele, for example, required a hit from a 15-inch shell to seriously damage them. Weapons were created to meet these needs (the 15-inch howitzer was a scaled-up version of the 9.2-inch, and became known, naturally, as "Granny"), but they were manned by British gunners and Royal Marines. The 9.2-inch howitzer, therefore, was the largest piece of ordnance in the Canadian Corps.

A Brilliant Canadian Lieutenant-Colonel
While Canada made virtually no contribution towards the design of the guns her troops were equipped with during the First World War, she was responsible for major advances in understanding their operation —and hence in how to use them more effectively in the field. In 1914, the concept of indirect fire was very new. Most senior gunners remembered when the dial sight was unknown and most targets were in plain view from the gun position. Speed into action was the first criterion, particularly with the Horse Artillery: fire could always be corrected by direct observation of the opening rounds. While this philosophy still had a role to play, even on the Western Front, it was unsuited to many of the conditions that prevailed and often to the effective accomplishment of missions that the artillery was called upon to perform.

55 Charles "Snaffles" Payne, *The Guns! Thank God! The Guns!"* coloured lithograph
  A unit of the Royal Horse Artillery is seen galloping into action.

56 Senior Canadian artillery officers on the Rhine, 1918. Brigadier-General A.G.L. McNaughton is second from left.

It was clearly difficult to achieve surprise if batteries had to carry out preliminary ranging (or registration) on their targets in advance. Similarly, if a barrage was to provide the advancing infantry with maximum support at minimum risk, accuracy of fire was of critical importance. A detailed study of the problems of applied ballistics that were involved became urgent. It was fortunate for Canada, and for the Commonwealth armies on the Western Front, that Lt.-Col. A. G. L. McNaughton accepted the challenge and solved many of the problems.

From his position as Counter Battery Staff Officer, Canadian Corps, McNaughton—when bombardments were being carried out without the benefit of correction by observers—had analysed the many factors that could cause the mean point of impact of a series of rounds to be other than on target. He found the first source of error to be in the maps themselves, which were often based on old French surveys. If the Canadian battery and the enemy gun positions were both hundreds of yards away from where the map showed them to be, the chances of silencing the opposition by "shooting from the map" were clearly remote. Given more accurate surveys, McNaughton turned his attention to the guns and their ammunition. Soon the statistics began to flow to his office. From these he pinpointed sources of error ranging from "lack of training and care in calculating and applying Initial Corrections [for the effect of abnormal meteorological conditions, gun wear, etc.] to Storage of [propellant] Charges under unsatisfactory conditions, to lack of sorting charges by Lots and Shell by Type and Driving Band, and to incorrect adjustment of Sights."* Some of the problems were beyond the control of the gunners in the field, and McNaughton called for more attention by the Department of Munitions "to the standardization of Type and uniformity of manufacture of Shells, Driving Bands and Propellants."*

As a gun barrel wears, the velocity of the shell as it leaves the muzzle begins to fall. In the case of an 18-pounder firing at a range of 8,000 yards, for example, this could mean the loss of about 300 yards in range during the life of the gun. The problem was that no two barrels performed

---

*A.G.L. McNaughton, *Analysis of Shoots by Canadian Corps Artillery, 1917–1918* (First Canadian Army in the Field, 1943), p. 5.

in the same way, and the correction figures in the Range Tables were based on broad averages. McNaughton had not been trained as an electrical engineer for nothing. He was aware of the instrument known as the Boulengé electrical chronograph (see p. 40). With it he could assess the time a shell took to pass through two wire screens carrying electric currents and located on carefully measured bases in front of the gun. Given this time span and knowing the ballistic coefficient (or the ability of the projectile to overcome air resistance), it was possible to compute the actual muzzle velocity. Prior to important actions, McNaughton arranged for many of his key guns to be individually calibrated at a test site equipped with Boulengé chronographs. This was typical of the meticulous and scientific approach to gunnery that characterized the Canadian Corps during the last two years of the war. The unorthodox spirits of the Royal Flying Corps cooperated willingly with this unusual Canadian soldier-scientist. They observed and recorded data on thousands of rounds fired by McNaughton's guns, enabling him to make surprising discoveries and to reverse many established beliefs. He found, for example, that when it came to predicted (programmed) fire, the 60-pounder was more accurate than any of the heavy howitzers. This was not the result of any inherent accuracy of the gun, but because the flight time of its shell to a given target was much shorter than that of the lower-velocity howitzers. Reports on the prevailing atmospheric conditions—or Meteor Reports, as they were known—were not particularly accurate. Therefore, the longer the projectile was in flight and thus subject to these influences, the greater was the chance of erroneous corrections being applied.

The Canadian success at Vimy in April 1917 owed much to McNaughton's work, but it was during the last two months of the war that his methods reached full fruition. The capture of Cambrai by the Canadian Corps in October 1918 was made possible by what is still a textbook example of artillery preparation. To approach Cambrai, the Canadians had to cross the barrier of the Canal du Nord. A short stretch of the canal (4,000 yards) was dry, and through this funnel the Canadian commander passed 50,000 men with tanks, guns and transport. The narrow avenue of assault was protected—magnificently—by artillery. Less than a month later, the Canadians captured Valenciennes, a key point in the defensive Hermann Line, strongly fortified and held by three German divisions. It was the final and most striking demonstration of McNaughton's philosophy of trying to win battles with accurate gunfire and not with the lives of men. The Canadian Corps fired almost as much ammunition in this engagement as had been used by both sides combined throughout the South African War. The cost in Canadian casualties was 80 killed and 300 wounded. The Germans lost the town, more than 800 dead, and 1,800 prisoners. The significance of the contribution that McNaughton and his colleagues had made to scientific gunnery was thus fittingly demonstrated in the last battle Canada was to fight in France during World War I.

**Peace and Yet Another War:
Canada Comes of Age**

5

57 (p. 84) Charles Fraser Comfort, *25-Pounder Firing* (detail), watercolour, 1944 (Coll.: Canadian War Museum)

The weapon is Canadian, in action near Cortona, Italy, during the winter of 1943-44.

58 Q.F. 25-pounder gun/howitzer (Coll.: Canadian War Museum)

Canada's Industrial Miracle

Between the end of the First World War and the outbreak of the Second, there was no more than a twenty-year period of peace. Isolationism, and a belief that the 1914–1918 struggle had been a war to end all wars, meant that Canada was poorly prepared when war came again in 1939. While Germany, Italy and Japan were on the march, Canada, believing she lived in a "fire-proof house", neglected her armed forces.

There certainly was no indication in 1939 that Canada would eventually provide half the naval escorts for the sustained Battle of the Atlantic; a powerful airforce that included fighter, bomber and coastal command squadrons; and the First Canadian Army, the first field army in Canada's history. Her sailors, airmen and soldiers were to serve in Europe, North Africa and the Far East in this global conflict. At home, Canadians manufactured aircraft, ships, tanks, trucks, guns, infantry weapons and ammunition in enormous quantities. The industrialization of Canada was taken a long step forward during the war years.

Technological changes came rapidly— from propeller-driven aircraft at the beginning to jets in the final days of the war. Radar, growing ever more sophisticated, helped win the Battle of the Atlantic and contributed massively to the success of the Allied bomber offensive over Germany. The weapons of destruction grew more powerful as guided missiles supplemented long-range artillery. Nuclear bombs, fortunately developed by the Allies, sent up mushroom clouds over Japan to signal the final phase—the victorious ending of the Pacific War.

As for artillery, Canada was to start the war with a conventional weapon—the 18-pounder gun of the First World War—but, as happened in every other field, more effective weapons were to replace it.

Between Wars: A New Artillery Piece

If the decision of a single statesman gave the Canadian Corps of the First World War one of the best field guns of the day, the Canadian army of the Second World War can be said to have got a vastly better field piece through the indecision of many politicians. Between the two world wars the guns of the Royal Canadian Artillery had changed but little from those the regiment had manned in France. The only significant innovation was the gradual introduction of mechanization. Dozens of trucks of various types eventually replaced hundreds of horses. But the guns were the same. In Britain, the question of a replacement for the 18-pounder gun and the 4.5-inch howitzer had been under consideration for many years. Such agreement as there was seemed to favour a single weapon that would be capable of carrying out the roles of both the relatively flat-trajectory, high-velocity gun and the high-trajectory, low-velocity howitzer. Again, there seemed to be some sort of agreement that the calibre should be somewhat more than 4 inches, with a shell weighing approximately 30 pounds. As it turned out, both the Germans and the Americans came to rather similar conclusions; the only difference was that they put their new 105-millimetre field pieces into production.

Technical difficulties were not the only problems British gun designers had to cope with; equally significant were the pervasive effects of economic depression and disarmament. A few experimental models of potential replacements were built, but it was clear that the politicians would never agree to the wholesale re-equipment of the Royal Artillery as their predecessors had done after the South African War. The only acceptable design would be one that, in some way or other, utilized the vast existing stocks of 18-pounders. These guns already had a calibre of 3.3 inches: with high-quality steel they could be more thinly relined to yield a calibre of 3.45 inches and thus permit the firing of a 25-pound shell. Out of these compromises and limitations came the famous 25-pounder gun/howitzer, generally recognized as the best all-round divisional field piece of any of the combatants in the Second World War. The original 18-pounder carriage placed severe restrictions on both the traverse (the side-to-side movement of the barrel) and the elevation that could be obtained. A new split-trail design took care of the elevation, but the problem still remained of providing sufficient traverse to enable the gun to take on an anti-tank role when needed. The eventual solution was found in a proposal that had been put forward at the end of the First World War. A circular platform was developed to be carried under the trail, and when the gun went into action the platform was dropped, thus providing a circular runway for the wheels and the effect of a full 360 degrees of traverse.

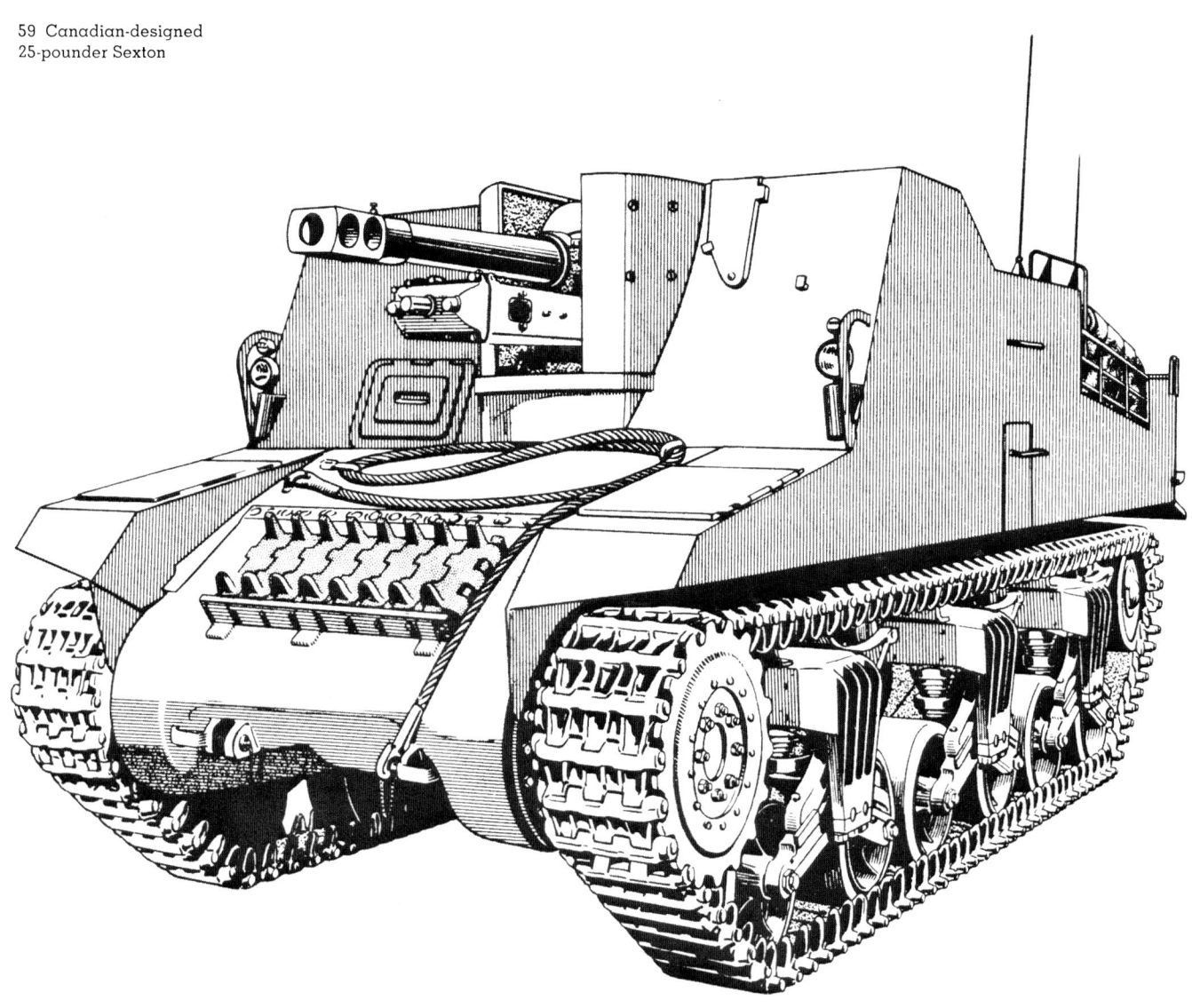

59 Canadian-designed 25-pounder Sexton

The majority of the converted 18/25-pounders having been lost at Dunkirk, the well-known contour of the final 25-pounder on its field carriage became the symbol of Canadian and British field batteries; many of the weapons were produced in Canada. As the war developed, the need for greater mobility and protection of the gunners led to the development of self-propelled 25-pounders. Canada made a considerable contribution here. The basis of the design was the chassis of the Ram, Canada's ill-fated attempt to design and produce a battle tank of its own. The Ram offered few advantages and numerous disadvantages as a tank, but stripped down and fitted with a 25-pounder it became the Sexton. This self-propelled weapon began to be introduced into both the Canadian and British armies in 1943, but it replaced only a small percentage of the towed guns on their field carriages.

The multitudinous roles planned for the new 25-pounder gun/howitzer called for more complicated ammunition than that used with the 18-pounder. As far as shells were concerned, the long-standing argument about the respective virtues of shrapnel and high explosive had finally been resolved in favour of the latter. But there still had to be carrier shells of many types to disseminate everything from screening smoke to propaganda leaflets. As a defence against tanks, a solid armour-piercing shot weighing 20 pounds was carried. The propellant charges became increasingly complex as new field requirements arose. It was clear from the beginning that more than one charge would be needed to provide the desired range and trajectories.

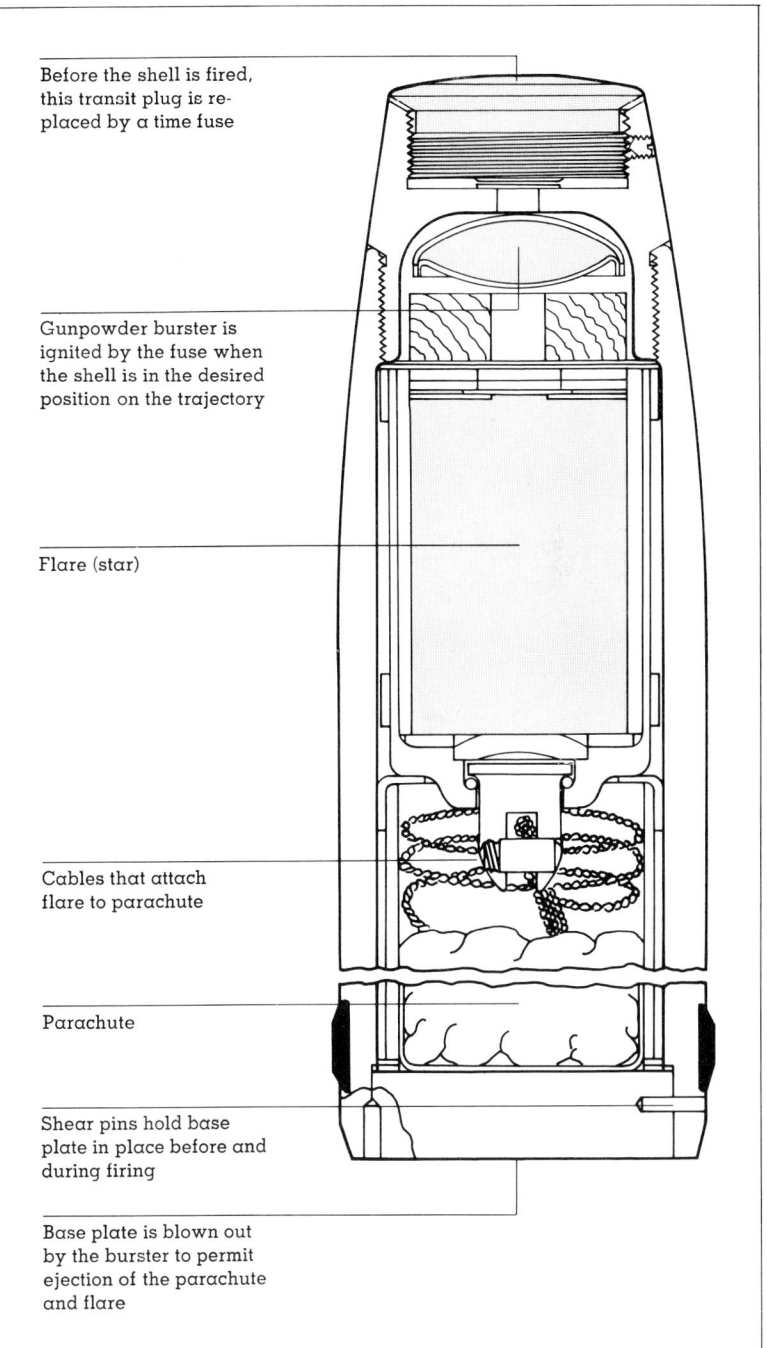

60 Components of a 25-pounder star shell, a typical carrier shell

61 Charles Fraser Comfort, *Canadian 5.5-Inch Guns*, watercolour, 1944 (Coll.: Canadian War Museum)

B.L. 5.5-inch gun/howitzer in action in Italy, 1944.

This necessitated the separate loading of ammunition, with the shell being rammed home before the cartridge case was loaded. A removable cup in the mouth of the case permitted the extraction of some of the propellant if less than full charge was required. Originally there were three charges, but extra increments introduced later provided greater ballistic flexibility. The inevitable call for more range than the designers had originally contemplated led to super-charge cartridges. By the time the gradual process of development had been completed, there was little doubt that what the 25-pounder had lost in weight of shell it more than made up in range and flexibility when compared to its 105-millimetre competitors, of both friend and foe. Before the war ended some Canadian regiments had, for logistic and related reasons, been issued with American 105-millimetre howitzers, but regret was mixed with nostalgia when they said farewell to their faithful 25-pounders.

More New Artillery

One of the two principal weapons of the Canadian Medium Artillery regiments of the Second World War had a direct link with its forerunner of the earlier war. The first of the new breech-loading 4.5-inch guns were, in fact, relined 60-pounders. Although their 55-pound shell was rather lighter than that fired by their famous predecessor, they achieved a significant increase in range. The ballistic flexibility provided by a choice of three propellant charges, and the capability of engaging targets at ranges in excess of 20,000 yards, made the breech-loading 4.5-inch gun a very useful weapon.

The other medium equipment of the Canadian army was designed, like the 25-pounder, to have the characteristics of both a gun and a howitzer. The immediate objective was a replacement for the 6-inch 26-hundredweight howitzer, which, while the most accurate of the heavier howitzers, lacked the range needed in modern warfare. A breech-loading 5.5-inch weapon that fired a 100-pound shell to a range of 16,000 yards solved the problem (an 80-pound shell was subsequently introduced). The availability of five propellant charges enabled virtually any target within range to be engaged, irrespective of the intervening terrain.

The carriage of the breech-loading 5.5-inch gun/howitzer, which also accepted the 4.5-inch gun, had a contour that was novel by British and Canadian standards. The split-trail design permitted achievement of the high elevations needed for both long-range fire and certain howitzer-type roles; but it was the two horn-like balancing springs, rising almost vertically above the barrel, that made the carriage distinctive. The springs were required because the trunnions (the two lugs cast with the barrel that permit it to pivot up and down) were much farther to the rear than in traditional British designs. Springs of this type were relatively common in European and Russian weapons, and, once the departure from custom had been accepted, the carriage was found to be well suited to the needs of the two guns it mounted.

New Targets: The Tank

During the Second World War, Canadian gunners faced two types of targets that, while not unknown to their counterparts of the previous generation, were of vastly more significance. These were tanks and aircraft: to attack them now demanded totally different techniques and equipment.

Although Britain had invented the tank, and had been the first country to demonstrate its potentialities, the interwar years saw its case being argued by only a small group of enthusiasts in the British army. Relatively few devoted any serious concern to the defeat of enemy tanks; the high-explosive shell of a field gun was considered adequate for the purpose. Such confidence was not altogether misplaced because the armour of both the British and German tanks of 1939–40 did not exceed 30 millimetres in thickness, comparable to that of the German tanks of 1918. The 2-pounder anti-tank gun, designed to handle this sort of target, was quite adequate for the job, and in fact was superior to the corresponding German 37-millimetre weapon. In the middle thirties, 30 millimetres of armour was seen by the British War Office as the likely upper limit. Neither they nor the gun designers foresaw that within ten years they would have to confront the 15-centimetre sloping plate of the German Tiger tanks.

62 Canadian 6-pounder anti-tank gun in Italy, 1944

63 Q.F. 17-pounder anti-tank gun (Coll.: Canadian War Museum)

The solid shot of the little 2-pounder had done a creditable job in France in May 1940. Not only was the enemy armour relatively thin, but the ranges were comparatively short. A very different situation arose in North Africa, where there was soon a desperate need for a heavier weapon. The response was the 6-pounder 7-hundredweight gun, which began to come into service towards the end of 1941. Still the German tanks grew in size and their armour in thickness. The next move was up to the British gun designers, whose answer was the 17-pounder, which appeared in the Mediterranean theatre in 1943. In both its towed and self-propelled versions, this powerful weapon became the standard equipment of the Canadian Anti-Tank regiments during the European campaigns of 1944–45. But even the 17-pounder could not defeat its heaviest adversaries by the kinetic energy of a solid steel shot. Fortunately, an effective alternative had been developed just in time to meet the need. Canadian research, again assisted and encouraged by A. G. L. McNaughton, now a general, played its part in keeping this gun ahead in the critical race with the enemy, through its contribution to the development of a new type of projectile—the British A.P.D.S.

64 Cross-section of a sabot projectile, showing the tungsten-carbide core (Coll.: Canadian War Museum)

65 German 20/28-mm anti-tank gun with tapered barrel (Coll.: Canadian War Museum)

66 The principle of the Littlejohn adapter

67 A Composite-Rigid anti-tank shot

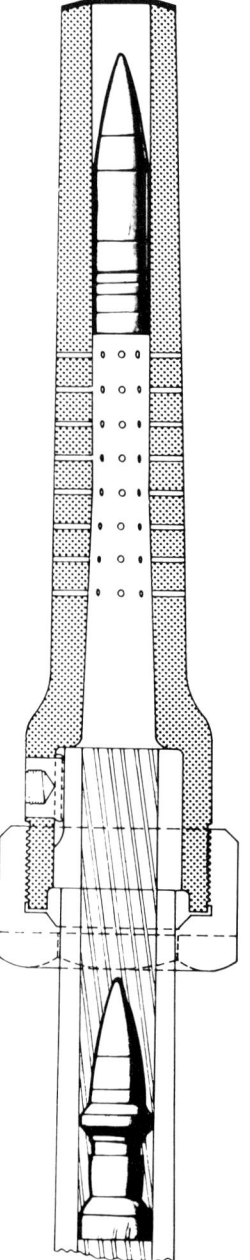

The essential elements of Armour-Piercing Discarding Sabot ammunition were the use of tungsten carbide instead of steel in the projectile, together with the achievement of very high muzzle and striking velocities by special attention to both internal and external ballistic problems. Tungsten carbide had long been known as a very effective penetrator of armour, and the French had planned to use it in ammunition in 1939. It was so much denser than steel, however, that a normal tungsten-carbide projectile of full-bore diameter would have been so heavy that it could only be fired at a relatively low muzzle velocity. One solution, which the Germans tried with considerable success, was to produce guns with conical (tapered) barrels that used ammunition composed of small tungsten-carbide cores surrounded by flanges, which were squeezed inwards as the shot moved down the tapering bore, with the result that the core itself never touched the bore. One of these German guns, which had been captured in North Africa, occasioned considerable surprise when tested at Woolwich; it was found to give muzzle velocities in excess of 4,000 feet per second, about double the muzzle velocity of a standard (untapered) piece. The British achieved a similar effect by adding a conical attachment (called the "Littlejohn adapter", from the translated name of its Czechoslovakian inventor, Janecek) to the muzzle of the 2-pounder gun. Both of these solutions, while reasonably efficient from a ballistic point of view, had the disadvantage of being incompatible with full-calibre high-explosive shells. Of course the Littlejohn adapter could be removed, but this was not always convenient and, even worse, was likely to be forgotten.

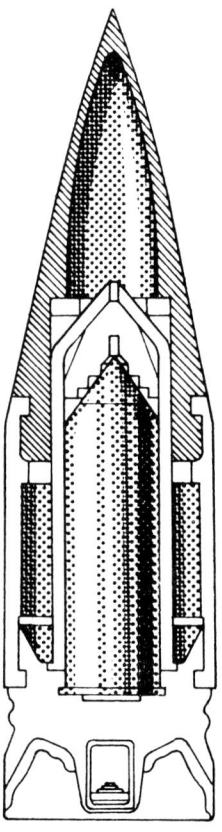

Neither the Composite-Rigid (C.R.) nor the High-Velocity Armour-Piercing (H.V.A.P.) types of round gave rise to the compatibility problem, but as they consisted essentially of a tungsten-carbide core in a lightweight body, their external ballistic characteristics were poor. The ballistic coefficient of a projectile determines its ability to overcome air resistance. If it is high, the drop in velocity along the trajectory is relatively low. This is obviously what is required for the defeat of armour by kinetic energy. Other things being constant, the ballistic coefficient increases with the weight of the shot, but decreases as the diameter of the projectile increases; these dimensions are critical. The C.R. round was relatively light but of full-bore diameter, with the result that its striking velocity fell rapidly as the range to the target increased. The A.P.D.S. round was also of full-bore diameter in the gun, but at the muzzle the small-but-heavy tungsten-carbide core separated from the base (a carrier shoe, hence "sabot") and the petal-like supports that had guided it during its passage down the barrel; the small-diameter projectile, now freed of its shoe, proceeded to the target with a ballistic coefficient much superior to that of a comparable C.R. shot. It is of interest to note that Canadian mastery of the "sabot" principle led eventually to a great peacetime achievement when, in the 1960s, the 16.5-inch gun of the McGill University High-Altitude Research Project (HARP)* fired "Martlet" research vehicles to ranges and altitudes greater than have ever been reached by any gun in history. Altitudes of ninety miles were reached. If the Martlets could be fitted with rocket boosters, they could place satellites in orbit at far less cost than can a purely rocket system.

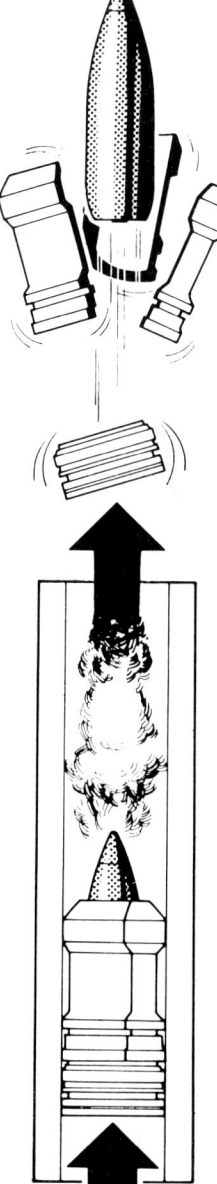

68 The principle of the discarding sabot projectile

*For further information on the project, see Leslie W.C.S. Barnes, "Project HARP: Into Space from a Gun", Discovery, Jan. 1965, pp. 39–42, 50.

69 The sabot principle applied to space research. This is one of the Martlet vehicles designed at McGill University, Montreal, leaving the muzzle of a 16.5-inch smooth-bore gun.

The blithe assumption that the close burst of a high-explosive shell from a field gun would disable any tank was soon disproved, and with it the prevailing doctrine of anti-tank defence by low-velocity weapons. In some cases, such as the 25-pounder, solid shot and a propellant charge designed to wring the maximum performance out of the gun was sufficient.

In due course, however, it became obvious that an alternative to kinetic energy would be needed. Again, the principle that was adopted long preceded its application. The "Munroe effect" offered the possibility of a substitute in the form of chemical energy. A thin-walled shell filled with a high explosive and fitted with a metal cone in its nose was able to produce and focus a jet of hot gas of considerable armour-piercing potential. This High-Explosive Anti-Tank (H.E.A.T.) round provided even the most unlikely weapons with a credible anti-tank performance.

70 Penetration of armour by the jet from a hollow-charge shell

71 The main features of a high-explosive hollow-charge anti-tank shell

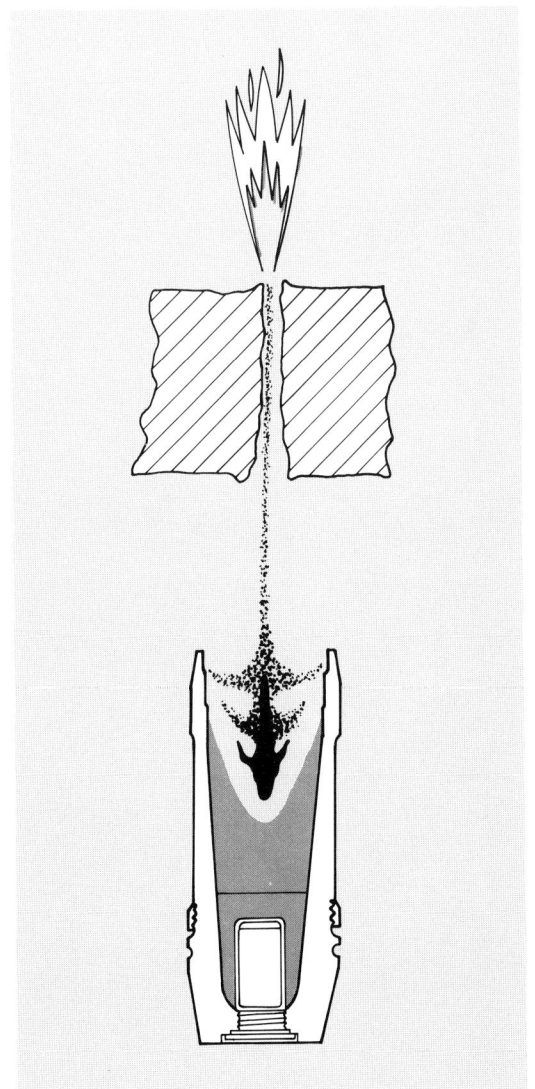

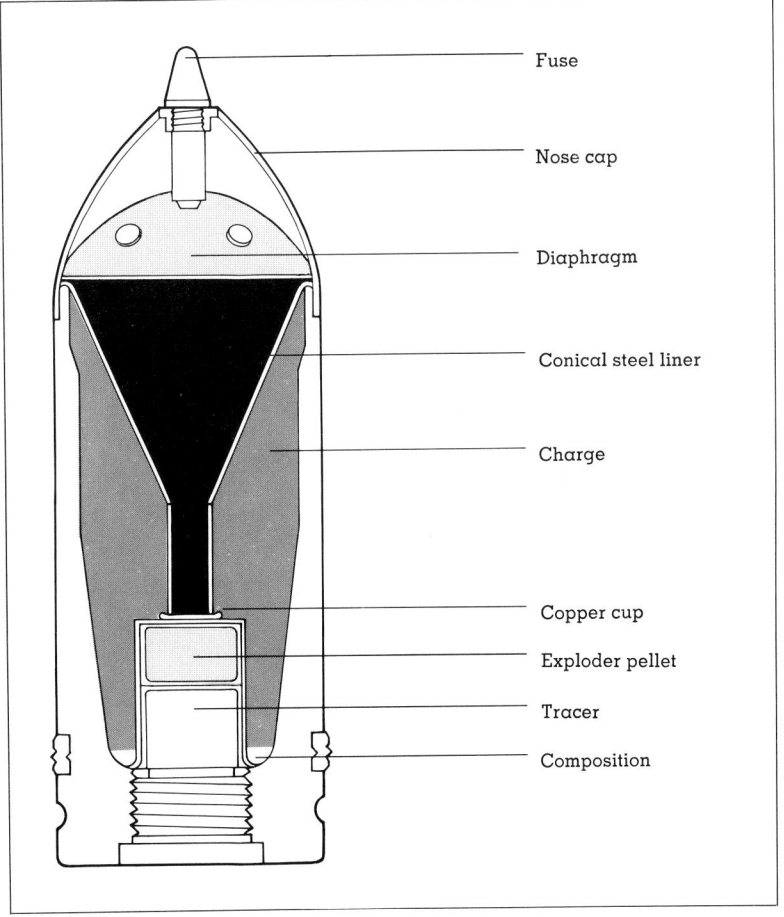

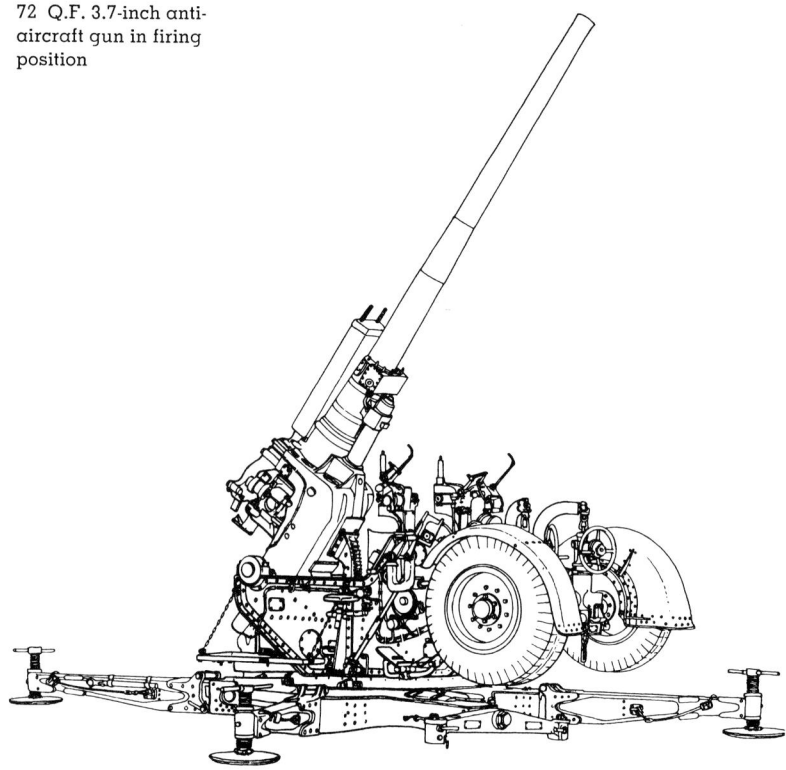

72 Q.F. 3.7-inch anti-aircraft gun in firing position

New Targets: The Aeroplane

Anti-aircraft fire was commonplace throughout most of the First World War, but the majority of the guns employed were essentially low-angle weapons fitted to makeshift high-angle mountings. The 3-inch 20-hundredweight gun was the only significant example in the Canadian Corps of a weapon designed primarily for anti-aircraft fire. It was effective during the First World War and remained in service to protect certain installations in Canada well into the Second. By that time, however, its low ceiling and its 12.5-pound shell made it of little use against the fast, high-flying aircraft of the day. The main weapon of the Canadian Anti-Aircraft regiments overseas was the British 3.7-inch gun, which was capable of firing a 28.5-pound shell to an altitude of over 30,000 feet. This gun, which began to enter service at the time of the Munich crisis, was in every way the equal of the famous German 88-millimetre gun of Western Desert fame. The only problem was that it took the British War Office longer than the German General Staff to see the potential of a powerful anti-aircraft gun in an anti-tank role.

There was one gun that was almost equally well known in the armies on both sides of the conflict. Interestingly enough, it was designed and initially built by a private firm in a neutral country, Sweden. The Canadian Light Anti-Aircraft regiments were thus in widely diversified company with their Bofors quick-firing 40-millimetre automatic guns. These weapons are a textbook example of a brilliant design with considerable capacity for ongoing development. The Swedish firm produced the first version of this gun in the late 1920s, Canada began to manufacture them in the autumn of 1940, and today its descendants are still to be found in dozens of countries throughout the world. Its 40-millimetre high-explosive shell was fitted with a sensitive percussion fuse. To avoid the unpleasant consequences that could have arisen from the shells missing their target and falling to earth in friendly territory, the tracer in the rear contained a self-destruction element that detonated the shell after a flight time of about seven seconds. This limited the effective ceiling of the gun, but was the unavoidable consequence of the fusing system. It fell to the Third Light Anti-Aircraft Regiment to score the Canadian Artillery's first kill with the new gun. On the night of 6 August 1941, on the Essex coast, a troop from the Sixteenth Battery opened fire on a German dive-bomber that had been caught by criss-crossing searchlights and sent it crashing into the sea.*

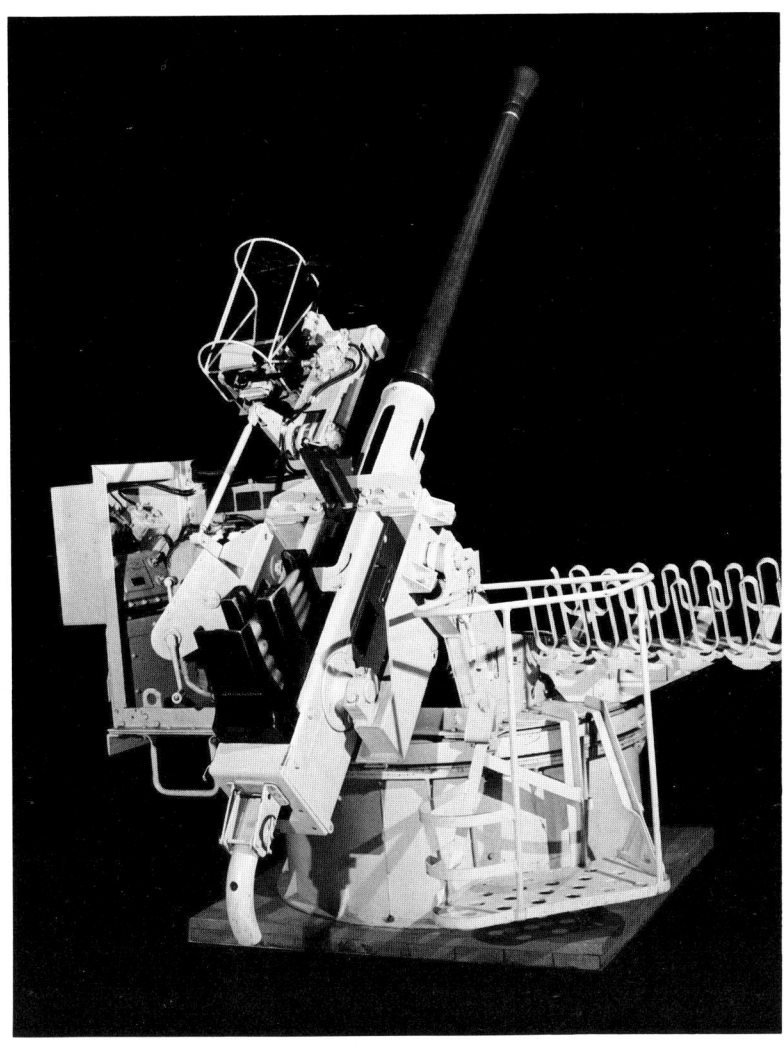

73 Q.F. 40-mm Bofors anti-aircraft gun on a static mounting, naval in this case (Coll.: Canadian War Museum)

*Nicholson, vol. 2, p. 77.

74 B.L. 9.2-inch coastal defence gun near Halifax, January 1941

Coastal Defence

There was one role—coastal defence—in which the guns of 1945 were virtually the same as those of 1918. In fact, guns so employed were already quite venerable when Canada went to war in 1914. The defence of Canada's ports and harbours rested mainly on two types of guns, the breech-loading 6-inch Mark VII and the breech-loading 9.2-inch Mark X. These excellent pieces were developed early in the century, and their quality was such that when the Canadian Coast Defence forts were closed during the 1950s they were willingly accepted by several North Atlantic Treaty powers as valuable additions to the defence of their own ports and naval bases. During their fifty years or so of Canadian service these guns, like most others, had their performance improved by the introduction of new charges, ballistically more efficient shells, and mountings that permitted firing at higher elevations (which achieved greater range).

The demands of war led to requirements for coastal-defence installations at many new locations, especially after Japan's entry into the war. Even the existing defended areas of long-established fortresses, such as Halifax and Esquimalt, had to be enlarged. The demand far outstripped the supply of coastal-defence guns, and it was necessary to resort to some rather unorthodox expedients. Field guns ranging from some of the earliest-model 18-pounders to American-manufactured versions of the French *soixante-quinze* were emplaced in many lonely outposts. In other locations, 6-pounders of South African War vintage carried out useful functions in halting shipping for examination. The main defences of the port of Saint John, New Brunswick, included three venerable breech-loading 7.5-inch guns at Mispec Battery. The story was that these were naval pieces that had been in storage at Halifax since the British cruiser they were intended to re-equip had been sunk a quarter of a century earlier. There was no doubt that ammunition for these veterans was exceedingly scarce; as none of them could be spared for transfer to a proof and experimental establishment, the tests required to evaluate alternative Canadian propellant charges were carried out at Mispec. Thus, the battery remained there,

ready to carry out its counter-bombardment role should any adventurous seaborne enemy threaten Saint John.

The only time that enemy shells fell on Canadian soil during the Second World War was in June 1942, when a surfaced Japanese submarine shelled the wireless station and lighthouse at Estevan Point, Vancouver Island. There were no batteries of coastal guns in the vicinity, so that the shelling, which fortunately caused no casualties and little damage, went unanswered.

The Perfection of Rocketry

Canadian initiative and determination played a significant part in restoring the rocket to land warfare during the final year of the 1939–1945 war. The various successors to the Congreve rocket fell into disuse with the advent of rifled guns during the latter part of the nineteenth century. The potentiality of rocket barrages as a means of anti-aircraft defence had been foreseen by the British during the 1930s, and the roar of 2-inch and 3-inch U.P.s (Unrotated Projectiles) became well known to many Canadian troops stationed in England during the Blitz. It was Canadian pressure, however, that led to the introduction of 5-inch rockets in a role reminiscent of the historic bombardment of Boulogne during the Napoleonic Wars. The rockets, each of which carried a warhead comparable in explosive content to a medium artillery shell, were fired in ripples from simple launchers known as Land Mattresses, and ranges of up to 8,000 yards could be achieved with acceptable accuracy. The first few dozen of these rockets were fired by the Canadians in November 1944 in support of the crossing of the River Scheldt, vital to the freeing for use of the Port of Antwerp—the largest port on the Continent and one that the Allies badly needed for their continued operations in northwestern Europe. From its small beginning, the use of this modern version of "ammunition without ordnance" grew rapidly. In Operation Veritable, during the Reichswald Battle, the First Rocket Battery Royal Canadian Artillery fired nearly six thousand rounds.

75 Test firings of Land Mattresses carried out by the First Canadian Rocket Battery in Belgium, October 1944, showing rockets in flight

76 Experiment with muzzle brakes at the Artillery Proof and Development Establishment, Valcartier, Quebec, 1943

As the war dragged on and the users called for ever-greater performance from their guns, it was found that the limiting feature of the existing weapons was often the carriage rather than the barrels. If some means could be found of reducing the violence of recoil, the muzzle energy could be increased and so, of course, could the velocity, range and striking power. Once more the solution was found in a principle that had been known for many years. The deflection of some of the muzzle gases to the rear could be used to generate forces acting in an opposite direction to the recoil, and hence to reduce the stresses on the carriage or mounting. Muzzle brakes produced for this purpose became increasingly common attachments, particularly on tank, anti-tank and field guns.

Propellants, Projectiles and Ever-Higher Explosives

One of the most significant developments in gunnery during the Second World War was the introduction of various flashless propellants. The tactical necessity for eliminating, or at least significantly reducing, the blinding flash associated with the firing of the traditional cordites at night grew dramatically in the years just prior to 1939. As an example, fast, high-flying aircraft could take avoiding action long before the shells reached them if they could see the flashes of the hostile anti-aircraft guns. The need was for propellant ingredients that would produce muzzle gases less liable to spontaneous ignition. The answer was found in nitroguanidine, or picrite. Propellants containing fifty per cent or more of this material generated large quantities of inert nitrogen, and were essentially flashless in many guns. Even when N-type (Nolight) propellants did not eliminate the flash, they had the distinct advantage of reducing the erosion of the bore, and hence of extending the life of the gun, in contrast to the erosiveness characteristic of traditional cordites. This was largely because flashless propellants burned in the barrel at a much lower temperature than that associated with the older compositions, with their high nitroglycerine content.

As the composition of the gun propellants changed, so did their physical shape. It was found, for example, that better performance could often be obtained from tubes rather than the traditional cords. When Canadian gunners began to receive increasing quantities of single-base propellants (consisting in the main of nitrocellulose) to American formulations, they noticed that the shape had changed yet again: short cylinders, pierced by six small holes, took the place of cords and tubes.

The new shape meant that, as the propellant burned in the gun, the surfaces available to liberate gas actually increased slightly as the projectile moved down the bore. In the case of cords, the surface decreased; and tubes, at their theoretical best, gave only a constant burning surface. The multi-tube shape produced a more sustained pressure on the shell, although it often had the minor disadvantage of being more difficult to ignite in a regular and reliable manner, and longer and more complicated primers had to be introduced.

The chemists not only gave Canadian gunners new propellants, they also provided high explosives significantly more powerful than those which had been available in 1914–1918. The most important of these new shell-fillings was RDX (so named for the Research Department at Woolwich, where it was developed). More powerful even than picric acid, RDX was too sensitive to be used in its pure form. Combined with forty per cent of TNT, it was known as Composition B. Even in this somewhat diluted form it was not only more powerful than existing high explosives, but it also possessed a very high velocity of detonation, which contributed to the development of a more effective pattern of fragments from the body of the shell it occupied.

77 Flashes from Q.F. 3.7-inch anti-aircraft guns firing at night

78 Cross-section of a Canadian-made No. 11 percussion primer, showing the magazine filled with black powder to aid propellant ignition

79 Cross-section of a No. 117 percussion fuse produced in Canada

Propellants and high-explosive fillings alone could not bring about the destruction of a target unless the shell was detonated by a reliable fuse. The sensitivity of percussion fuses improved over the years, and the accuracy of powder-burning fuses and clockwork time-fuses became the object of constant research between the wars. But it was the advent of the V.T. (Variable Time) proximity fuse that changed many aspects of gunnery. This fuse, a British invention developed for production by the Americans, was in essence a tiny radar set that detonated the shell when it was close to the target—which could be an aircraft, a trench line, or advancing enemy troops. By the end of the war, these fuses became increasingly available to both Canadian anti-aircraft and field batteries.

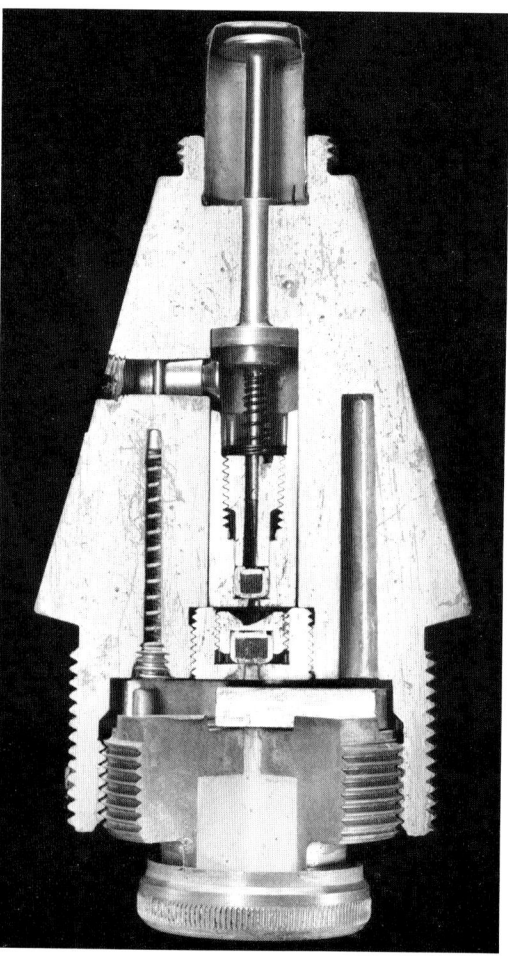

Canada: Arms Factory to the Free World

During the winter of 1943, the workers in a gun factory at Sorel, Quebec, heard a recording made by a CBC war correspondent in Italy. It was of thunderous gunfire —the voices of more than two thousand guns of the Eighth Army heralding the opening of the Battle of the Moro River in Italy. But the record carried a further message of special interest to the workers. The commentator told them that most of the guns they could hear preparing the way for the advance of the great Commonwealth army of Canadian, British, Indian and New Zealand troops had been built in their factory. The guns of Canada had achieved a new dimension of significance.

By the time the Second World War was over, the Western Allies had produced nearly fifty million rounds of heavy and medium artillery ammunition. Twelve per cent of these were made in Canada. The total production of field, tank and anti-tank ammunition was almost ten times larger, and Canada contributed seven per cent of this vast quantity. Canada built six per cent of the 177,000 artillery weapons produced between September 1939 and June 1945—almost one-sixth of British production and rather more than one-tenth of the output of the United States. Viewed in the light of both the relative size of Canada's industrial base and her almost complete lack of previous experience in modern armament manufacture, this was an outstanding performance.

80 Manufacture of 25-pounders at Sorel, Quebec, July 1941

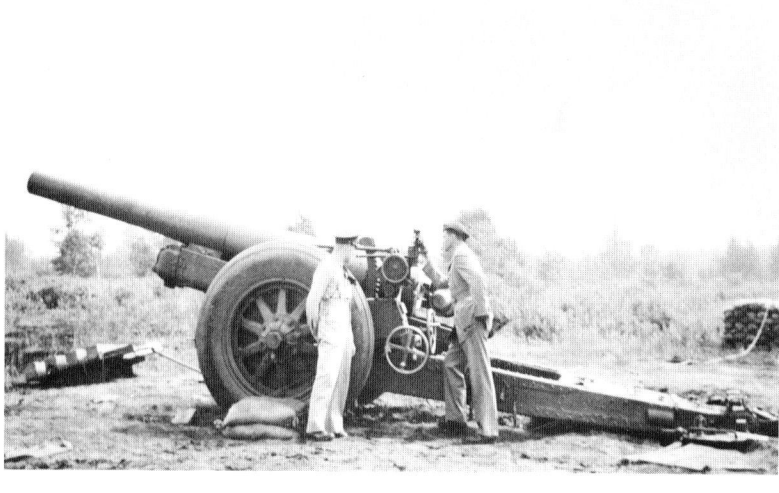

81 Testing Canadian-made B.L. 7.2-inch howitzer ammunition at the Valcartier proof ranges, 1943

Before the war, as the dark shadow of Hitler's power had spread over Europe, the politicians of Britain and Canada did little more than procrastinate about establishing gun and ammunition production facilities in Canada. The British Government believed that the urgent needs of rearmament would be met most effectively by using the limited funds available to expand the existing British armament industry. Ottawa would not undertake the building of a reserve production potential without the guarantee of large orders and heavy capital investment by Britain. Such breakthroughs as did occur were often the result of the initiative of individual Canadian industrialists who sought and won British contracts. An example is Edouard Simard of Sorel, Quebec, a member of the family that created one of the largest industrial organizations in the province; before the war he obtained a contract to manufacture one hundred 25-pounder guns. When Canada declared war on Germany in September 1939, the only artillery ammunition being produced, other than the trickle from the Dominion Arsenal in Quebec, was a few thousand empty 3.7-inch shells a week. As for explosives, Canada promised 150 tons of TNT a month—by Christmas.

All in all, it was hardly a major contribution to the needs of a Commonwealth at war. During the first fifteen months of hostilities, Canada supplied only three per cent of the munitions received by the forces of the Commonwealth. Ninety-one per cent came from Britain and six per cent through purchases from the then neutral United States.

The whole scope and pace of Canadian war production began to surge forward following the fall of France. All other considerations gave way to the struggle for freedom. A United Kingdom Technical Mission was established in Ottawa, and soon contracts were being placed, inspection and development facilities were being planned, and liaison was being developed with the recently established Canadian Department of Munitions and Supply.

Figures alone cannot measure the true significance of Canada's eventual output, but they are impressive by any standards. A sample might include 17,000 complete guns and 50,000 barrels, 23 million rounds of anti-aircraft ammunition, 150,000 tons of propellants and a similar quantity of TNT, 33,000 dial sights, and 14 million armour-piercing shot.

The proof-testing of guns and ammunition is an essential corollary of armament production. Its history is almost as old as the art of gunnery itself. Early in the Second World War it was decided that Canada's main proof and experimental establishment would be set up on the site of the old First World War range at Valcartier, Quebec. The characteristics of the site were far from ideal, the choice having been dictated more by historical inertia and political expediency than by technical considerations. Nevertheless, by 1943, the Artillery Proof and Development Establishment, which was then under the control of the Joint Inspection Board of the United Kingdom and Canada, had been developed into a major facility that subsequently formed the nucleus around which the postwar Canadian Armament Research and Development Establishment of the Defence Research Board was to grow.

82 Canadian-built Q.F. 6-pounder 7-cwt. anti-tank guns being tested at the Valcartier proof ranges, 1943

A network of proof ranges, of which Valcartier was the technical centre, served the main production areas of the country from Hamilton, Ontario, to Longueuil, Quebec. In the years from 1941 through 1945, these ranges fired more than 1,750,000 rounds. This total included not only production evaluation and control, but also a steadily increasing experimental and research programme. One of the natural features of Valcartier was turned to advantage to assist in improving the cold-weather performance of guns and ammunition. Tests showed some zinc alloys—cheap and convenient to use in ammunition components—to be dangerously brittle when fired at low temperatures. It was also noted that cold weather was liable to seriously influence the performance of some types of ammunition. Sometimes the results were undesirable variations in muzzle velocity and, in extreme cases, the occurrence of dangerously high pressures in the gun chamber. Tackling, and usually solving, these and many other problems arising from production and from user experience became commonplace at Valcartier. New propellants were tested; McNaughton's "sabots" were evolved; improved ballistic instrumentation was designed; and, all the while, the ultimate test of proof-firing checked the safety and acceptability of the great flow of guns and ammunition that Canada poured into the Allied war effort around the world.

In this account we have seen that Canada not only manufactured guns in the Second World War, but had kept pace with—and also developed—new technology. And the products of her factories had been used superbly by her gunners overseas (53,000 officers and men) as well as by her Allies.

It is perhaps appropriate to end this book with the 25-pounder gun, whose manufacture was getting under way in Canada even as war broke out, for it was a 25-pounder of the First Royal Canadian Horse Artillery that fired what was the last shot from a Canadian gun during the Second World War. This was in the Netherlands on the afternoon of 3 May 1945, when a German mortar was engaged. As the smoke cleared and the barrel completed its cycle of recoil and recuperation, a great chapter in the story of Canada's guns came to an end. A few years later the guns were to speak angrily again in Korea; since then, they have continued to play their role in the North Atlantic Treaty Organization and in United Nations' peacekeeping operations throughout the world. Wellington's hard-pressed infantrymen cried "The guns—thank God—the guns!" Canada today has reason to be similarly grateful.

Suggested Reading List

Three books that trace the history of the gun in broad outline are:

Batchelor, John, and Ian Hogg. *Artillery*. New York: Ballantine, 1973.

Rogers, H.C.B. *Artillery Through the Ages*. London: Seeley, 1971.

Wilson, A.W. *The Story of the Gun*. 3rd ed. Woolwich, England: Royal Artillery Institution, 1968.

Anyone seeking more detailed studies of early weapons might consult:

Hogg, O.F.G. *English Artillery 1326–1719*. London: Royal Artillery Institution, 1963.

Hughes, B.P. *British Smooth-Bore Artillery: The Muzzle-Loading Artillery of the Eighteenth and Nineteenth Centuries*. London: Arms and Armour Press, c. 1969.

Canadian weapons production is referred to in:

Hall, H. Duncan. *North American Supply*. London: Her Majesty's Stationery Office and Longmans, Green, 1955.

Hitsman, J. Mackay. *Military Inspection Services in Canada, 1855–1950*. Appendix by W.M. Thomson. Ottawa: Queen's Printer, 1962.

Two books that might be of interest to those seeking more detailed information on some of the principles involved in gun and ammunition design are:

Great Britain, Ministry of Supply, Scientific Advisory Council. *Internal Ballistics*. Ed. by F.R.W. Hunt. London: His Majesty's Stationery Office, 1951.

Read, John. *Explosives*. Middlesex, England: Penguin, Pelican Books, 1942.

Anyone wishing to know more about a fascinating organization that influenced much of our story over the centuries should refer to:

Skentelbery, Norman. *Arrows to Atom Bombs: A History of the Ordnance Board*. London: Her Majesty's Stationery Office, 1975.

The guns of Canada cannot be studied in isolation from the men who manned them in peace and war. We are fortunate in having their story told so well in:

Nicholson, G.W.L. *The History of the Royal Regiment of Canadian Artillery*. 2 vols. Toronto: McClelland and Stewart, vol. 1, 1967; vol. 2, 1972.

And those who would like to know more about General A.G.L. McNaughton, the greatest gunner that Canada has ever produced, are directed to his biography:

Swettenham, John. *McNaughton*. 3 vols. Toronto: Ryerson, vol. 1, 1968; vols. 2 and 3, 1969.

Index

Abel, Frederick, 62
Abraham, Plains of, 28, 32, 36
Aix-la-Chapelle, Treaty of, 32
Alesia, Siege of, 14
Ammunition
    Canadian production of, 76–7, 104, 106–7
    fixed, 34, 69
    premature explosion of, 71, 75
    shortages of, 71, 75
    See also Ballistics; High Explosives; Projectiles; Propellants
Antwerp, 101
Armstrong, William, 53–4
Artillery (word), 19
Artillery, types of
    Early:
    bombard, 19–20, 22
    cannon, 14, 23
    Dulle Griete (Mad Meg), 20
    King's Daughters, 19
    Mohammed's great gun, 20
    Mons Meg, 19, 20
    mortars, 14, 23, 26
    peterara, 21
    pot-de-fer (vasi), 18, 19, 23, 26
    17th, 18th Centuries:
    guns:
        field, 28, 32–3, 35, 36, 38, 41
        naval, 30, 31
        siege, 30, 32
    howitzers, 32, 36, 37
    mortars, 30, 32, 36, 37, 41
    19th Century:
    carronades, 24
    guns:
        breech-loading, 54, 57; 6-pdr. (Armstrong), 54; 12-pdr. 6-cwt., 62–3
        quick-firing, 57, 61
        rifled, 53–5, 60; R.M.L. 7-pdr., 56; R.M.L. 9-pdr., 55–6, 62; R.M.L. 64-pdr., 56; R.M.L. 12-in. (Palliser), 57
        smooth-bore, 52, 53, 55, 56; 3-pdr., 46, 50, 56; 6-pdr., 50, 52, 100; 9-pdr., 49, 52; 18-pdr., 53; 24-pdr., 47; 32-pdr., 56
        soixante-quinze (75-mm), 59
    mortars, 36, 47
    20th Century:
    anti-aircraft weapons, 98–9, 102, 103
    anti-tank weapons, 91–4, 97, 107
    coastal-defence weapons, 100–1

    guns:
        breech-loading: B.L. 4.5-in., 90, 91; B.L. 6-in. Mark VII, 100; B.L. 7.5-in., 100; B.L. 9.2-in. Mark X, 100; B.L. 60-pdr., 77, 78, 83, 90
        Ehrhardt 15-pdr., 68
        quick-firing: Q.F. 3-in. 20 cwt., 98; Q.F. 3.7-in., 98, 103; Q.F. 37-mm, 91; Q.F. 40-mm (Bofors), 98–100; Q.F. 88-mm, 98; Q.F. 2-pdr., 91, 93, 94; 6-pdr. (German), 92–3, 107; Q.F. 13-pdr., 68, 69–70; Q.F. 17-pdr., 92–3; Q.F. 18-pdr., 64, 66, 69–70, 74, 82, 86–7, 100
        soixante-quinze (75-mm), 68, 100
        20/28-mm anti-tank, 93
    gun/howitzers:
        B.L. 5.5-in., 90–1
        25-pdr., 84, 86, 87, 89–90, 97, 105, 106, 108; self-propelled (Sexton), 88–9
    howitzers:
        breech-loading: B.L. 6-in. 26-cwt., 78, 79, 90; B.L. 6-in. 30-cwt., 78; B.L. 7.2-in., 106; B.L. 9.2-in. ("Mother"), 80, 81; B.L. 15-in. ("Granny"), 81; Big Bertha (42-cm), 19, 77; Schlanke Emma, 77
        quick-firing: Q.F. 4.5-in., 74, 87; 105-mm (American & German), 87, 90
    Land Mattress (rocket launcher), 101
Artillery Proof and Development Establishment, 76, 102, 107–8
Austrian Succession, War of the, 30

Bacon, Roger, 18, 25
Bagley, Mathew, 24
Ballista, 16, 17, 18
Ballistics, 39–40, 42, 82–3, 94–5, 108
Baltimore, 52
Barbed wire, cutting of, 71–3
Batoche, Battle of, 56
Battering ram, 16
Battles, see names of individual battles
Bergen-op-Zoom, siege of, 26
Bladensburg, Battle of, 52
Blenheim, Battle of, 36
Boer War, *see* South African War
Bonifacio, siege of, 60
Boulengé, Captain Paul-Émile, 40
Boulengé chronograph, *see* Electrical chronograph
Boulogne, bombardment of, 51, 101
Bowmen, 16, 22, 53
Boxer, Colonel E.M., 60

Brackenbury, Sir Henry, 68–9, 70
Breech, closure of, 21, 57
Breech-loading, 24, 54, 57
Brock, Sir Isaac, 46–7
Brown, Jacob, 50
Bureau brothers, 20
Byng [of Vimy, Viscount], 13

Cambrai, capture of, 83
Canadian Army
    19th Century:
    field batteries, 55, 62
    Permanent Force, 55
    South African War: 63, 66–7
    First World War:
    Canadian Artillery, 70, 79
    Canadian Corps, 13, 77, 81, 82, 83, 87, 98
    Field Artillery brigades, 74
    First Canadian Division, 80
    heavy batteries, 78
    siege batteries, 78
    67th Battery, C.F.A., 66
    Second World War:
    anti-aircraft batteries, 104
    Anti-Aircraft regiments, 98
    Anti-Tank regiments, 93
    field batteries, 104
    First Canadian Army, 86, 87
    First Canadian Rocket Battery, 101
    gunners overseas, 108
    Medium Artillery regiments, 90
    Royal Canadian Horse Artillery, 108
    Third Light Anti-Aircraft Regiment, 99
Canal du Nord, 83
Carleton, Sir Guy, 13
Carriages, gun, 23, 34, 47, 62–3, 70, 78, 87, 89, 91, 102
Carron iron works, 24
Cartier, Jacques, 13
Catapult, 16, 18, 19
Charles II, 42
Charles VII (France), 20
Churchill, Sir Winston, 67–8
Coeur, Jacques, 20
Congreve, Sir William, 51
Congreve, William (son of Sir William), 51
Congreve rocket, 50–2
Constantinople, siege of, 20, 27
Corsica, 22, 60
Crécy, Battle of, 19, 22
Crimean War, 53
Crysler's Farm, Battle of, 44, 50
Cut-Knife Hill, Battle of, 56

De Bange obturator, 57
Defence Research Board (Canada), 107
Detonators, 60–1. See also Fuses
Detroit, 46
Dewar, James, 62
Dominion Arsenal, 76, 106
Dunkirk, 89

Edward III, 19, 22
Eighth Army (British), 104
Electrical chronograph, 40, 42, 83
Elevation of guns and howitzers, 34, 36, 63, 70, 74, 87, 91
Estevan Point, Vancouver Is., 101

First World War, 66, 68–83
Fish Creek, Battle of, 56
Formigny, Battle of, 22
Frontenac, [Comte de], 30, 31
Fuses
  early, 26, 47–9
  percussion, 60–1, 72, 99; No. 44, 72; No. 106, 73; No. 117, 104
  time and percussion: No. 56, 62; No. 80, 72, 75, 76
  Variable Time proximity, 104

Gibraltar, siege of, 18, 47
Gun (word), 19
Gun-making, 53–4, 59, 69, 75, 87
  brass in, 23–5, 30, 46, 50, 52, 59
  bronze in, 24, 35, 56
  in Canada, 86, 89, 104–7
  iron in, 20–1, 25, 30, 54, 59
  steel in, 59, 69
Gunpowder, see Propellants, types of
Guns, see Artillery, types of
Gustavus Adolphus (Gustavus II of Sweden), 34

Henry IV, 19
Henry V, 19
Henry VIII, 25
Hermann Line, 83
High-Altitude Research Project (HARP), 95, 96
High explosives
  Composition B, 103
  gunpowder, 61
  picric acid (lyddite), 61, 103
  RDX, 103
  trinitrotoluene (TNT), 61, 103, 106, 107
  See also Ammunition
Howard, Edward, 60

Howitzer (word), 36
Howitzers, see Artillery, types of
Hundred Years' War, 20
Hutton, Charles, 40

India, 51, 56
Indians, North American, 13, 30
Industrial Revolution, 52
Inkerman, Battle of, 53

James II (Scotland), 21
Janecek, 94
Joint Inspection Board of the United Kingdom and Canada, 107

Key, Francis Scott, 52
Kingston, Ont., 49
Kirke, Sir David, 30
Korea, 108

Laurier, Sir Wilfrid, 63
Leipzig, Battle of, 52
Leliefontein, action at, 63
Littlejohn adapter, 94
Loos, Battle of, 71
Louisbourg, sieges of, 30, 32
Lundy's Lane, Battle of, 50

McGill University, 95, 96
Mackinac Is., 46
McNaughton, A.G.L., 13, 81, 82–3, 93, 108
Madison, James, 46
Marignano, Battle of, 22, 23
Marlborough, John Churchill, 1st Duke of, 23, 36, 42
"Martlet", 95–6
Merbury, Nicholas, 19, 23, 42
Middle Ages, 18, 22
Middleton, Sir Frederick, 56
Minden, Battle of, 36
Mons, retreat from, 70
Montcalm, [Marquis de], 32
Montgomery, Richard, 13
Moro River, Battle of the, 104
Mortars, see Artillery, types of
Munitions (Britain), Ministry of, 77, 82
Munitions production
  Britain, 75
  Canada, 76–7, 86, 89, 104–7
Munitions and Supply (Canada), Department of, 107
Munroe effect, 97
Muzzle-loading, 24, 43, 52, 54, 55, 57
Muzzle velocity, see Ballistics

Napoleon, 53, 59
Neuve Chapelle, Battle of, 71, 80
Newfoundland, 47, 48
North Atlantic Treaty Organization, 100, 108
Northwest Rebellion, 56

Operation Veritable, 101
Ordnance, Board of, 42–3, 51
Ordnance Works, Coventry, 74, 80

Palliser, William, 55
Palliser's gun-rifling system, 55–7
Passchendaele, Battle of, 64, 81
Peacekeeping operations, 108
Peninsular War, 49
Pepys, Samuel, 60
Phips, Sir William, 30, 31
Pikemen, Swiss, 22
Primers, 103
Projectiles, types of
  Early:
  case shot (canister), 13, 27, 47
  darts, iron, 18, 26
  grapeshot, 13, 27, 47
  rockets, 18
  shells, mortar, 26
  shot: iron, 26, 53; stone, 20, 26
  18th, 19th Centuries:
  rockets, Congreve, 50–2, 101
  shells: elongated, 53, 55; studded (Palliser), 55
  shot, red-hot, 47
  Shrapnel "spherical case-shot", 47–50
  20th Century:
  guided missiles, 86
  nuclear bombs, 86
  rockets (Unrotated Projectiles), 101
  shells:
    anti-aircraft, 98–9, 106
    carrier, 89
    high-explosive, 70, 71–3, 89, 94, 97, 103
    High-Explosive Anti-Tank (H.E.A.T.), 97
    hollow-charge, 97
    shrapnel, 70, 71, 74, 76–7, 89
    13-pdr. gun, 69
    18-pdr. gun, 69, 70
    25-pdr. gun/how., 89, 90
    4.5-in. how., 74, 87
    5.5-in. gun/how., 90, 91
    9.2-in. how., 80
  shot:
    anti-tank, 89, 93–4, 97
    Armour-Piercing Discarding Sabot (A.P.D.S.), 89, 93–5, 107
    Composite-Rigid (C.R.), 94, 95
    High-Velocity Armour-Piercing (H.V.A.P.), 95
  See also Ammunition

Proof-testing of guns and ammunition, 24, 57, 76, 106, 107–8
Propellants
   Canadian production of, 107
   ignition of, 26, 60–1, 103
   ingredients of:
      nitroglycerine, 62, 102
      nitroguanidine (picrite), 102
   types of:
      cordite, 62
      flashless (N-type), 102
      gunpowder, 18, 22, 25, 26, 34, 61
      nitrocellulose (*Poudre B*), 62, 102
   variable charges, 74, 78, 89–90
   See also Ammunition

Quebec, attacks on, 13, 28, 30, 31, 32
Queenston Heights, Battle of, 47, 49

Radar, 86, 104
Recoil
   principle, 58–9
   control systems, 68–9
      axle spade, 62, 63
      muzzle brakes, 102
Red River Campaign, see Northwest Rebellion
Reichswald Battle, 101
Robins, Benjamin, 39
Rockets, see Projectiles, types of
Rodman, Thomas J., 40
Roxburgh Castle, siege of, 21
Royal Field Artillery, 52, 53, 62, 68, 69
Royal George, HMS, 49
Royal Horse Artillery, 52, 53, 62, 68, 69, 81
Royal Regiment of Artillery, 42
Rumford, Count, see Thompson, Sir Benjamin
Russell Motor Car Company, 76

Sabot principle, 93–6
Saint John, N.B., 100–1
Scheldt, River, 101
Schwarz, Berthold, 18
Scotland, 19, 23, 24
Scott, Winfield, 49
Second World War, 85–108
Seringapatam, siege of, 51
Seven Years' War, 32, 36
Shells, see Projectiles, types of
Shrapnel, Henry, 47, 48, 51
Shrapnel shells, see Projectiles, types of (18th, 19th and 20th centuries)
Simard, Édouard, 106
Sorel, Que., 104, 105, 106
South African War, 63, 66–7, 70, 74, 83, 100
Spion Kop, Battle of, 67

Tanks
   German, 91, 93
   Ram (Canadian), 89
Thompson, Sir Benjamin, 39, 40
Thunderer, HMS, 57
Trebuchet, 18
Tungsten carbide, 94–5
Tyre, siege of, 16

Valcartier, Que., 76, 107, 108
Valenciennes, Battle of, 83
Velocity of shot, see Ballistics
Victoria Cross, 63
Vieille, Paul, 62
Vimy Ridge, Battle of, 12, 13, 73, 75, 83

War of 1812, 44–7, 49–50
Warkworth Castle, siege of, 19
War memorials
   Canadian National War Memorial (Ottawa), 66
   Royal Artillery Memorial (London), 80
Washington, D.C., 52
Waterloo, Battle of, 23, 49, 52, 53, 61, 66
Wealden iron works, 25
Wellington, Duke of, 23, 42, 43, 49, 59, 108
Western Front, 70, 78, 81–2
Whitworth, Sir Joseph, 54
Wolfe, James, 32, 36
Woolwich Arsenal, 40, 51, 55, 57, 69, 73, 77, 94, 103

York (Toronto), 49

Zizka, General, 23